FORTH Fundamentals
Volume 2
Language Glossary

Volume 1: Language Usage
Volume 2: Language Glossary

FORTH Fundamentals
Volume 2
Language Glossary

C. Kevin McCabe

dilithium Press
Beaverton, Oregon

10   9   8   7   6   5   4   3   2

Library of Congress Cataloging in Publication Data
(Revised for volume 2)

McCabe, C. Kevin.
    FORTH Fundamentals.

    Includes index.
    Contents: v. 1. Language usage — v. 2. Language glossary.
    1. FORTH (Computer program language)   I. Title.
QA76.73.F24M33 1983   001.64'24   83-7250
ISBN 0-88056-091-6 (v. 1)

Printed in the United States of America

dilithium Press
8285 S.W. Nimbus
Suite 151
Beaverton, Oregon 97005

In Memory of Jory Graham
Journalist, advocate, educator — and always my friend.

"A mind trained in the law can understand anything — except computers. If God had wanted lawyers to understand computers, he wouldn't have created paralegals."

The Wall Street Journal,
19 August 1983

Important Notice to Readers

FORTH is an evolving language, not yet standardized. This text is based primarily upon fig-FORTH, a version distributed in the public domain by the FORTH Interest Group, a nonprofit corporation dedicated to the advancement of the language. Fig-FORTH forms the basis for many micro/minicomputer FORTH variants, including FORTH-79, but does differ from some commercial versions of the language. The reader is strongly urged to study this text along with any available system and installation manuals, and to note any differences.

The author has made every effort to insure the accuracy of this text. However, the author, publisher, and distributors of this text shall not be liable for errors contained herein or for any loss, damage, or injury of whatever nature allegedly caused or contributed to by this material or by the negligence or fault of any person.

Volume 2 — Language Glossary

Introduction to Volume 2

For convenience, this text is divided into two volumes intended for concurrent use. Volume 1 introduces the major features of the FORTH language and describes and illustrates their use. This volume is a glossary and a detailed examination of the "core" fig-FORTH and FORTH-79 versions of the language. It includes listings of all core words, along with descriptions of parameter stack effects, usage formats, and execution effects. Also included are full annotations for all fig-FORTH words which are defined in terms of other FORTH words.

The user should be aware that FORTH is far from standardized.[1] As most commercially available versions of FORTH contain additional system-dependent functions, the user is strongly urged to consult all applicable system manuals in conjunction with this text. This glossary includes all words found in Release 1 of the fig-FORTH language model. Also included are the extensions implemented in Release 1.1 of fig-FORTH for the 8080/Z-80, and in the proposed standard FORTH-79's core and extension (double-precision number and assembler) vocabularies.[2]

Glossary entries are organized by word name, in ascending ASCII order. This means that words like ! (store) and : (colon) are listed before words that begin with a letter.[3] Each entry uses a common format:

WORD (Pronunciation)   < Vocabularies >

Stack Diagram

Usage Format

Execution Description

Volume 1 Reference

Colon Definition (Fig-FORTH Model)

The first line of each entry includes the word and the pronunciation (for any word which includes non-alphabetic characters or whose pronunciation might be ambiguous). FORTH-79 specifies a pronunciation for each core word, but fig-FORTH does not. When not specified by any fig-FORTH publication, pronunciations have been selected by the author and are without "official" sanction. The vocabulary which includes the word is shown at the end of the line, using the symbols shown in Table 1.

SYMBOL	CORE VOCABULARIES
f	Fig-FORTH model
s	FORTH-79 standard core
x	FORTH-79 standard extension
z	Fig-FORTH 8080/Z-80 extension

Table 1: Vocabulary Symbols

The stack diagram shows the word's stack usage. Some (though not all) FORTH words use or change the contents of the parameter stack.[4] A stack execution diagram uses the symbols in Table 2 to show the effects of these operations. For certain immediate words in the fig-FORTH core, two stack diagrams will be shown. The first diagram shows the actual stack effects of the immediate word when it is executed during compilation; the second diagram shows the effects of any later associated run-time procedure.[6] Note that many run-time words for FORTH-79 are not defined within the standard, and are not accessible to the user. Accordingly, compilation stack diagrams are applicable only to the fig-FORTH version of the word.

A number of FORTH words may only be used within colon definitions or in conjunction with other words. In such cases, the required format will be shown. Other words in the input stream

SYMBOL	STACK VALUES	DATA BITS	PADDING BITS
addr	Memory address	16	0
b	Byte	8	8
c	ASCII character	7	9
d	Signed double-precision number	31 + sign	0
f	Boolean flag	1–16	0–15
ff	Boolean false flag	1–16	0–15
n	Signed single-precision number	15 + sign	0
tf	Boolean true flag	1–16	0–15
u	Unsigned single-precision number	16	0
ud	Unsigned double-precision number	32	0

Table 2: Stack Value Symbols

which are essential to execution are designated by the symbols found in Table 3.

The execution description presents the accepted definition of the word, including any variations between the fig-FORTH and FORTH-79 versions. Where appropriate to a complete description, any associated run-time procedure utilized in the fig-FORTH version will also be described; note that FORTH-79 will not necessary use the same procedure.

The Volume 1 reference tells where in Volume 1 the word is described or illustrated. For example, 4.3 designates Section 4.3, and 4.3.2 denotes Example 4.3.2 in that section.

The colon definition for each word so defined in the fig-FORTH model is also shown, in annotated vertical format. The definition's components are shown at the left side of the line; comments on the execution effects of each component follow on the right. All numeric literals shown as components or used in the accompanying comments are specified in decimal form unless otherwise noted. Hexadecimal values will be explicitly indicated with a trailing "H" character.

SYMBOL	INPUT STREAM TEXT
< dname >	Defining word name
< name >	Word name
< vname >	Vocabulary defining word name
. . .	Unspecified or arbitrary word(s)

Table 3: Input Word Symbols

FOOTNOTES

[1] Debates—often heated, and never dull—over language extensions and changes seem to be part of every gathering of FORTH programmers. As the primary developer of the language has noted (see Appendix C, Volume 1), FORTH is a polarizing language, in part because it is one of the few ever fully developed by the "grassroots" efforts of ordinary programmers.

[2] Ragsdale, William F., Fig-FORTH Installation Manual, Glossary, and Model (Release 1.0, August 1980); Fig-FORTH For 8080 Assembly Source Listing (Release 1.1, September 1979); and FORTH Standards Team, FORTH-79 (October 1980). The contents of these public domain documents are utilized courtesy of the FORTH Interest Group, P.O. Box 1105, San Carlos, CA 94070.

[3] See Appendix A, Volume 1.

[4] The parameter stack is described in Chapter 1 of Volume 1.

[5] As shown in Section 1.4 in Volume 1, each symbol denotes a stack value, with the " > > > " indicating execution of the associated word. Symbols to the left of the " > > > " denote stack values that are used as operands and removed by execution; those to the right of the arrow are left on the stack as results of execution. Where more than one symbol appears on either side, the rightmost one of the group is the value on top of the stack.

[6] See Section 5.5, Volume 1.

Fig-FORTH and FORTH-79 Glossary

(null)   **<f>**

Immediate word to terminate interpretation of the input stream when it has been exhausted. The input stream may be either a line of text from the terminal or a screen of source code from the disk.

The name of this word is the ASCII null (00H), which is a non-printing character. A line of text input from the terminal by **EXPECT** or **QUERY** will have one or more null characters added at the end; a disk block buffer will be terminated by one or more nulls as well.

Execution of "null" causes the inner text interpreter loop (which parses, then executes or compiles, individual words) to terminate if input is from the terminal. If input is from mass storage, the inner loop terminates if the last block of the current source code screen has been interpreted; otherwise, the block number is incremented for another pass. Exit from the inner to the outer text interpreter loop re-initializes the return stack pointer and causes the next line of text to be accepted from the terminal.

Reference: 9.4, 12.2

Colon Definition:
```
: (NULL)
    BLK @                    Fetch the current block number. A
                             zero value denotes input from the
                             terminal; a non-zero value, input
                             from disk.
```

IF	True branch — input is from the disk.
1 BLK +!	Increment the disk block number.
0 IN !	Initialize the input offset variable.
BLK @	Fetch the number of the next block to be interpreted.
B/SCR	Leave the number of blocks per editing screen.
1 – AND 0=	Leave a true flag if the current block is the last one in the screen.
IF	True if input is from the last block.
?EXEC	Error if not executing.
R> DROP	Drop the pointer to the next word.
ENDIF	
ELSE	False branch — input from the terminal.
R> DROP	Drop the pointer to the next word.
ENDIF	
; IMMEDIATE	Terminate definition, set precedence.

◇   ◇   ◇

! (store)   <f,s>

Stack: **n addr** > > >

Store the number **n** in the cell (two bytes) beginning at **addr**.

Reference: 3.1

◇   ◇   ◇

!CSP (store-c-s-p)   <f>

Store the current stack pointer in user variable **CSP** for compilation error checking.

Colon Definition:
: !CSP

SP@	Fetch the stack pointer.
CSP !	Store the pointer in the user variable.
;	Terminate definition.

◇   ◇   ◇

(sharp)   <f,s>

Stack: **ud1** > > > **ud2**

Format: **< # ... # ... #>**

Generate the next digit in the pictured output text string. Double-precision number **ud1** is divided by the current input/output number base, leaving the quotient **ud2** for further processing. Execution places at least one digit in the text string.

Reference: 9.5

Colon Definition:
: #

BASE @	Fetch the current number base.
M/MOD	Divide **ud1** by the base, leaving a single-precision remainder and double-precision quotient **ud2**.
ROT	Rotate remainder to top of stack.
9 OVER <	Leave **tf** if remainder is 10 or more.
IF	True branch — digit uses a letter A-Z.
7 +	Add 7 to provide for conversion to an alphabetic rather than numeric ASCII character.
ENDIF	Terminate conditional.
48 +	Add 48 (30H) to convert to ASCII.
HOLD	Insert the digit's ASCII character into the output string.
;	Terminate definition.

◇   ◇   ◇

#> (sharp-greater)   <f,s>

Stack: **ud** > > > **addr n**

Format: **< # ... #>**

End conversion of an unsigned double-precision number. The first (leftmost) character of the resulting pictured output text string will be located at **addr**, and the string will have a length of **n** characters.

Reference: 9.5

Colon Definition:
: #>

DROP DROP	Drop remaining **ud** from the stack.
HLD @	Fetch the pointer to the latest text character.
PAD	Leave a pointer to the start of the text output buffer.
OVER –	Calculate character count **n**.
;	Terminate definition.

#BUFF (number-buff)   <z>

Stack: > > >**n**

System constant containing the number of mass storage buffers allocated in memory.

#S (sharp-s)   <f,s>

Stack: **ud** > > > 0 0

Format: **<# ... #S ... #>**

Generate the ASCII characters for the pictured numeric output text corresponding to double-precision number **ud**, character-by-character, until a double-precision zero remainder is found. At least one digit will be generated.

Reference: 9.5

Colon Definition:
: #S

BEGIN	Begin an indefinite loop.
#	Generate the next character, leaving a double-precision remainder on the stack.

OVER OVER	Duplicate the remainder.
OR 0=	Leave a true flag if the remainder is zero.
UNTIL	Repeat the loop until a true flag.
;	Terminate definition.

◇　　　◇　　　◇

' (tick)　　　　　　　　　　　　　　　　　　　　　　　　　　< f,s >

Stack: > > > **addr**　　　　　　　　　　　(run-time)

Format: ' < name >

　　Immediate word to leave the parameter field address of the next word < **name** > from the input stream. If < **name** > is not found in the searched vocabularies, an error condition results. Fig-FORTH searches include both the current and context vocabularies; FORTH-79 checks only the context vocabulary.

　　When encountered during compilation of a colon definition, "tick" is executed immediately due to its precedence bit. The parameter field address **addr** of < name > is removed from the stack and compiled as a literal into the next dictionary location.

Reference: 7.2, 7.5, B.1

Colon Definition:
: '

−FIND	Search for a match to the next word < **name** > in the input stream. If found, leave the parameter field address **addr**, length byte, and a true flag; otherwise, leave only a false flag.
0= 0 ?ERROR	Error if no match found.
DROP	If a match is found, drop the length byte.
[COMPILE] LITERAL	If compiling, compile **addr** as a literal into the next dictionary location.
; IMMEDIATE	Terminate definition, set precedence.

((paren)   **<f,s>**

Format: **(. . .)**

Immediate word to ignore the following text until a delimiting right parenthesis is detected. Used to place non-executed, non-compiled comments within the input stream or source code.

One or more spaces must follow **(** in the same manner as any other FORTH word. The right parenthesis character is merely a delimiter, not a word, and need not be separated from the comment by spaces.

Reference: 4.3.7, 5.5

Colon Definition:

: (

47 WORD	Place the next text string, up to the ")" delimiter (ASCII 47), at the top of the dictionary in the word buffer without resetting the dictionary pointer.
; IMMEDIATE	Terminate definition, set precedence.

(+LOOP) (run-plus-loop)   **<f>**

Stack: **n > > >**

Compiled by **+LOOP** in a colon definition as the run-time procedure to increment the loop index and check for termination.

When **+LOOP** is encountered during compilation of <**name**>'s colon definition, it executes immediately. This in turn causes compilation of **(+LOOP)** into <**name**>'s parameter field, along with an in-line offset back to the first word of the loop.

During later execution of <**name**>, **(+LOOP)** executes by using the signed value **n** to increment the loop index. If the loop is not completed, the in-line offset is used to transfer execution back to the start. If the loop is completed, the offset is ignored; execution continues normally after dropping the loop parameters from the return stack.

Reference: 5.5

(.") (run-dot-quote)   \<f\>

Compiled by **."** in a colon definition as the run-time procedure to send the following in-line text to the current output device.

Reference: 5.5

Colon Definition:
: (.")

R	Copy the pointer to the next word from the return stack. That location holds the count byte of the following dimensioned string.
COUNT	Leave a pointer to the first text byte and the count on the stack.
DUP 1+	Duplicate and increment the length.
R> +	Add the count to the pointer to the next word, to create the pointer to the next location after the in-line text.
>R	Move the incremented pointer to the return stack.
TYPE	Output the text string.
;	Terminate definition.

(;CODE) (run-semicolon-code)   \<f\>

Compiled by **;CODE** in a colon definition of defining word \<dname\> as the run-time procedure to rewrite the code field of the most recently defined word.

When **;CODE** is encountered during compilation of \<dname\>'s colon definition, it is immediately executed. This in turn causes compilation of **(;CODE)** into \<dname\>'s parameter field, along with the machine code which specifies the generic execution procedure for all words in \<dname\>'s class.

During later execution of \<dname\>, in the form
\<dname\> \<name\>

a new header is created for < **name** >. The last item in < **dname** >'s
execution is **(;CODE)**, which modifies the pointer in < **name** >'s
code field before returning control to the text interpreter. The new
code field will point to the generic execution procedure contained in
< **dname** >'s parameter field.

Reference: 8.3

Colon Definition:
: (;CODE)

R>	Copy the pointer to the next word from the return stack. That location and the ones which follow hold the generic execution procedure.
LATEST	Leave the name field address of the most recent definition in the current vocabulary.
PFA CFA	Leave the code field address of that definition.
!	Store the new code field pointer.
;	Terminate definition.

◇   ◇   ◇

(ABORT) (parens-abort)   < f >

Executes after an error if the value of user variable **WARNING**
is −1.

The procedure may be modified for particular processors or in-
stallations during assembly, or by rewriting the word's first parameter field pointer to point to the code field of another procedure.

Reference: 12.4

Colon Definition:
: (ABORT)

ABORT	Invoke the **ABORT** procedure.
;	Terminate definition.

◇   ◇   ◇

(DO) (run-do)   < f >

Stack: **n1 n2** > > >

Compiled by **DO** within a colon definition as the run-time procedure to move the loop parameters from the parameter stack to the
return stack.

When **DO** is encountered during compilation of < **name** >'s
colon definition, it is executed immediately due to its precedence
bit. This in turn causes compilation of **(DO)**into < **name** >'s parameter field.

During later execution of < **name** >, **(DO)**executes by moving
the loop's initial index and limit values from the parameter stack to
the return stack.

Reference: 5.5

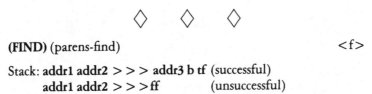

(FIND) (parens-find)   <f>

Stack: **addr1 addr2 > > > addr3 b tf** (successful)
     addr1 addr2 > > >ff   (unsuccessful)

Search a vocabulary, beginning at the name field address **addr2**,
for a match to the text string beginning at **addr1**. If a matching name
is found, leave the definition's name field address **addr3**, its length
byte **b**, and a true flag; otherwise, leave only a false flag.

(LINE) (parens-line)   <f>

Stack: **n1 n2 > > > addr n3**

Leave the address **addr** within the mass storage buffer area corresponding to the start of line **n1** of screen **n2**. The standard screen line
length **n3** is also left as a result. If the referenced line is not already in
memory, the appropriate block will first be read from the disk to a
buffer.

Reference: 11.2

Colon Definition:
: (LINE)
   >R   Move **n2** to the return stack.
   64 B/BUF   Leave the number of characters per
                           line and number of data bytes per
                           block.

*/MOD	Find the byte offset into the block, and the number of blocks above the start of the screen.
R>	Move the screen number **n2** back.
B/SCR * +	Find the block offset relative to the start of the current disk.
BLOCK	Leave the address within the buffer area of the first data byte of the block, after transferring the block into memory if needed.
+	Find **addr** by adding the offset to the start of the referenced line.
64	Leave the line length.
;	Terminate definition.

(LOOP) (run-loop)   <f>

Compiled by **LOOP** in a colon definition as the run-time procedure to increment the loop index and check for termination.

When **LOOP** is encountered during compilation of <name>'s colon definition, it executes immediately. This in turn causes compilation of **(LOOP)** into <name>'s parameter field, along with an in-line offset back to the first word of the loop.

During later execution of <name>, **(LOOP)** executes by incrementing the loop index by 1. If the loop is not yet completed, the in-line offset is used to transfer execution back to the start. If the loop is completed, the offset is ignored; execution continues normally, after dropping the loop parameters from the return stack.

Reference: 5.5

(NUMBER) (parens-number)   <f>

Stack: **d1 addr1 > > > d2 addr2**

Used by **NUMBER** to convert a dimensioned text string beginning at **addr1** into its numeric equivalent, using the current number base. Double-precision number **d1** serves as an accumulator, with the result being left as **d2**. A pointer **addr2** to the first unconvertible character is left on top of the stack.

See **CONVERT**.

Reference: 9.5

Colon Definition:
: (NUMBER)

BEGIN	Start an indefinite loop.
1+	Increment **addr1** to point to the next digit character.
DUP >R	Save one copy of the pointer on the return stack.
C@ BASE @	Fetch the next character and the current input/output base.
DIGIT	Convert the character, leaving the binary equivalent and a true flag on the stack. If conversion is not possible, leave only a false flag.
WHILE	If successful, continue loop.
SWAP	Exchange positions of the high-order half of **d1** and the binary equivalent of the character.
BASE @ U∗	Take the unsigned product of the base and the high-order half of **d1**.
DROP	Drop the high-order half of the product.
ROT	Move the low-order half of **d1** to the top of the stack.
BASE @ U∗	Multiply by the base value.
D+	Accumulate the double-precision total.
DPL @ 1+	Leave a zero if no decimal point, or a position number if detected.
IF	True branch—decimal point found.
1 DPL +!	Increment the pointer.
ENDIF	
R>	Move the pointer to the next digit character back to the stack.
REPEAT	Continue the loop until an unconvertible digit is found.

R>	Remove the address **addr2** of the first unconvertible digit from the return stack.
;	Terminate definition.

◇   ◇   ◇

* (times)   <f,s>

Stack: **n1 n2 > > > n3**

Leave the signed product **n3** of **n1** and **n2**.

Reference: 1.3.2, 2.2

Colon Definition:
: *

U*	Leave the unsigned double-precision product of **n1** times **n2**.
DROP	Drop the high-order half.
;	Terminate definition.

◇   ◇   ◇

*/ (times-divide)   <f,s>

Stack: **n1 n2 n3 > > > n4**

Leave the signed quotient **n4** of (n1*n2)/n3, using an intermediate double-precision product.

Reference: 2.2

Colon Definition:
: */

*/MOD	Leave the signed remainder and quotient.
SWAP DROP	Drop the remainder.
;	Terminate definition.

◇   ◇   ◇

*/MOD (times-divide-mod)   <f,s>

Stack: **n1 n2 n3 > > > n4 n5**

Leave the signed quotient **n5** and remainder **n4** of (n1*n2)/n3, using an intermediate double-precision product. The remainder **n4** has the same sign as the intermediate product.

Reference: 2.2

Colon Definition:
: */MOD
  >R   Move **n3** to the return stack.
  M*   Leave the signed double-precision
                                  product of **n1** and **n2**.
  R>   Move **n3** back to the parameter stack.
  M/   Perform the division, leaving the
                                  remainder and quotient.
  ;   Terminate definition.

◇   ◇   ◇

+ (plus)   <f,s>

Stack: **n1 n2** > > > **n3**

Leave the signed sum **n3** of signed numbers **n1** and **n2**.

Reference: 1.1.2, 1.3.3, 2.2

◇   ◇   ◇

+! (plus-store)   <f,s>

Stack: **n addr** > > >

Increment by **n** the 16-bit value stored in the cell (2 bytes) at **addr**.

Reference: 3.1

◇   ◇   ◇

+ − (plus-minus)   <f>

Stack: **n1 n2** > > > **n3**

Leave **n3**, with the magnitude of **n1** and the sign of **n1 * n2**.

Reference: 2.2

Colon Definition:
: +−
    0<   Leave a true flag if **n2** is negative.
    IF MINUS ENDIF   If true, negate the remaining value.
;   Terminate definition.

◇   ◇   ◇

+BUF (plus-buf)   <f>

Stack: **addr1** > > > **addr2 f**

Advance mass storage buffer address **addr1** to the address of the
next buffer at **addr2**, in sequence. If **addr1** points to the last buffer,
addr2 will point to the first buffer. Flag f is true only if **addr2** does not
match the address pointer in **PREV**.

Reference: 10.2

Colon Definition:
: +BUF
    B/BUF 4 +   Leave the disk buffer length.
    +   Add length to **addr1**, for **addr2**.
    DUP LIMIT =   True if **addr2** is the upper boundary
                                        of the mass storage buffer area.
    IF DROP FIRST ENDIF   If true, replace **addr2** with the address
                                        of the lower boundary.
    DUP   Copy the address.
    PREV @   Fetch the address of the most recently
                                        used mass storage buffer.
    −   Compare addresses by subtraction,
                                        and leave the result as a flag.
;   Terminate definition.

◇   ◇   ◇

+LOOP (plus-loop)   <f,s>

Stack: **n1** > > >   (run-time)
       addr n2 > > >   (compilation)

Format: **:** <**name**> ... **DO** ... **+LOOP** ... **;**

Immediate word to complete compilation of an indexed loop using an explicit index increment of **n1**.

During compilation of <**name**>'s colon definition, **+LOOP** executes immediately due to its precedence bit. In turn, a pointer to the run-time routine (**+LOOP**) is compiled into <**name**>'s parameter field. The **addr** operand, left by **DO**, is used to calculate and compile an offset back to the first word of the loop. The **n2** operand, also left by **DO**, is used for compilation error-checking.

During later execution of <**name**>, (**+LOOP**) executes by using the signed value **n1** to increment the loop index. If the loop is not completed, the in-line offset is used to transfer execution back to the top of the loop. If the loop is completed, the offset is ignored; execution continues outside the loop, after dropping the loop parameters from the return stack.

For positive values of **n1**, the loop terminates whenever the incremented index equals or exceeds the limit parameter. For negative values of **n1**, fig-FORTH terminates the loop when the incremented index is less than or equal to the limit value; FORTH-79 requires that the incremented index be less than the limit for termination, not merely equal to it.

Reference: 5.3, 12.4

Colon Definition:
: +LOOP

3 ?PAIRS	Test the error check value **n2**. If not equal to 3, issue an error message.
COMPILE (+LOOP)	Compile a pointer to the run-time routine into the next location in <**name**>'s parameter field.
BACK	Use **addr** to calculate the backwards offset to the top of the loop, and compile it into <**name**>'s definition.
; IMMEDIATE	Terminate definition, set precedence.

◇   ◇   ◇

+ORIGIN (plus-origin)   <f>

Stack: **n** > > > **addr**

Find an absolute address **addr** by adding **n** to the installation-dependent starting address of fig-FORTH in memory.

Reference: 6.2

, (comma)   <f,s>

Stack: **n> > >**

Compile the value **n** into the next cell (two bytes) at the top of the dictionary, and increment the dictionary pointer.

The value will be stored in binary format. The byte order within the cell is undefined, though most fig-FORTH systems place the high-order half of **n** in the cell's first byte.

Reference: 7.3

Colon Definition:

: ,

HERE	Leave a pointer to the next available location at the top of the dictionary.
!	Store **n** in the next dictionary cell.
2 ALLOT	Increment the dictionary pointer to point beyond the compiled value.
;	Terminate definition.

◇   ◇   ◇

– (minus)   <f,s>

Stack: **n1 n2 > > > n3**

Subtract **n2** from **n1**, and leave the signed result **n3** on top of the stack.

Reference: 1.4.4, 2.2

Colon Definition:

: –

MINUS	Reverse the sign of **n2**, with the same absolute magnitude.
+	Add the values.
;	Terminate definition.

-- > (next-screen)   <f>

Immediate word to end interpretation of a source code screen and begin interpretation of the next screen. Any words after **-- >** on the current screen will be ignored.

Reference: 11.4

Colon Definition:
: -->
?LOADING	Issue an error message if not loading.
0 IN !	Initialize the input offset pointer.
B/SCR BLK @	Leave the number of blocks per screen, and fetch the current block number.
OVER	Copy the number of blocks per screen to the top of the stack.
MOD – BLK +!	Increment and store the new block number.
; IMMEDIATE	Terminate definition, set precedence.

–DUP (dash-dup)   <f>

Stack: **n > > > n**   (n equals zero)
     n > > > n n   (non-zero n)

Leave two copies of the top stack value **n** if **n** is non-zero, or only one if **n** equals zero.
   See **?DUP**.

Reference: 1.4

Colon Definition:
: –DUP
DUP	Copy **n** for use as a flag.
IF DUP ENDIF	If true (non-zero), copy **n** again.
;	Terminate definition.

−FIND (dash-find)   <f>

Stack: > > > **addr b tf**   (match found)
    > > > **ff**   (not found)

Copy the next blank-delimited word < **name** > from the input stream to the word buffer at the top of the dictionary, with a preceding length byte. Both the current and context vocabularies are searched for a matching word name. If a match is found, the word's parameter field address and length byte are left on the stack below a true flag. If no match is found, only a false flag is left on the stack.
    See **FIND**.

Reference: 7.5, 12.2

Colon Definition:
: −FIND

BL WORD	Copy the next blank-delimited word to the word buffer, with a preceding length byte.
HERE	Leave a pointer to the next available location at the top of the dictionary.
CONTEXT @ @	Fetch the name field address of the most recent addition to the context vocabulary.
(FIND)	Search the designated vocabulary.
DUP 0=	Duplicate the flag, and reverse the top flag.
IF	True branch — no match found.
DROP	Drop the other flag.
HERE	Leave a pointer to the next available location at the top of the dictionary.
LATEST	Fetch the name field address of the most recent addition to the current vocabulary.
(FIND)	Search the designated vocabulary.
ENDIF	Terminate conditional.
;	Terminate definition.

◇   ◇   ◇

–TRAILING (dash-trailing)   <f,s>

Stack: **addr n1 > > > addr n2**

Examine the characters of a dimensioned text string whose **n1** text characters begin at **addr**. Adjust the stack value to **n2** to ignore all trailing blanks. The contents of the string's preceding count byte are not changed.

For FORTH-79, the operand **n1** must be zero or greater.

Reference: 9.2

Colon Definition:
: –TRAILING

DUP 0	Copy the initial count **n1**, and use it and a zero as loop parameters.
DO	Begin an indexed loop.
OVER OVER	Duplicate **addr** and the count.
+ 1 –	Calculate the address of the rightmost unexamined character.
C@	Fetch the character.
BL –	Compare with a blank, by subtraction.
IF LEAVE	If true (non-blank), leave the loop at the end of the current pass.
ELSE 1 –	If false (blank found), decrement the count on top of the stack.
ENDIF	Terminate conditional.
LOOP	Repeat the loop until the rightmost non-blank character is located.
;	Terminate definition.

◇   ◇   ◇

. (dot)   <f,s>

Stack: **n > > >**

Output a signed single-precision value **n** to the terminal, followed by one space. A preceding negative sign will be printed if the most significant bit of **n** is set to 1.

Reference: 1.1.2, 1.2, 2.1, 3.3

Colon Definition:

: .

S–>D	Convert **n** to its double-precision equivalent.
D.	Output the value and a space.
;	Terminate definition.

◇   ◇   ◇

." (dot-quote)   <f,s>

Format: **."** ... "

Immediate word to output the following in-line text, up to a delimiting "quote" character, to the terminal. Neither the space after **."** nor the trailing "quote" are printed.

When **."** is encountered during compilation of a colon definition, it is executed immediately due to its precedence bit. A pointer to the run-time routine associated with **."** is compiled, followed by the text string in dimensioned format. During later execution of the new definition, the run-time routine will output the text string.

When **."** is encountered during execution, the text string will be immediately output.

For fig-FORTH, there may be an installation-dependent maximum string length. FORTH-79 permits at least 127 characters, which must not include a "return".

Reference: 1.1.1, 3.3, 4.3.5, 5.5, 7.2, 7.3, 9.2, 9.3

Colon Definition:

: ."

34	Leave the ASCII code of the delimiter.
STATE @	Fetch the compilation state flag.
IF	True branch—compiling.
COMPILE (.")	Compile a pointer to the run-time routine into the next dictionary location.
WORD	Copy the following characters, up to a trailing delimiter, from the input stream to the word buffer.

HERE C@	Fetch the count byte contents.
1+ ALLOT	Adjust the dictionary pointer to point beyond the text string.
ELSE	False branch—executing.
WORD	Copy the following characters, up to a trailing delimiter, from the input stream to the word buffer.
HERE	Leave a pointer to the count byte.
COUNT	Adjust the pointer to the first text byte and leave the count on the stack.
TYPE	Output the characters.
ENDIF	Terminate conditional.
; IMMEDIATE	Terminate definition, set precedence

.CPU (dot-c-p-u)   < z >

Output the processor identification, stored as a base 36 value (digits 0-Z) in four bytes within the boot-up literal area.

.LINE (dot-line)   < f >

Stack: **n1 n2 > > >**

Output line **n1** of source code screen **n2** to the terminal. Trailing blanks will not be output.

Reference: 11.2

Colon Definition:
: .LINE

(LINE)	Leave the address within the mass storage buffer area corresponding to the first character of line **n1** of screen **n2**, and the standard line length. If not already in memory, the block containing line **n1** will first be read from the disk.
−TRAILING	Adjust the character count to ignore trailing blanks.

| TYPE | Output the string. |
| ; | Terminate definition. |

◇   ◇   ◇

.R (dot-r)   <f>

Stack: **n1 n2 > > >**

Output the value **n1** to the terminal, right-justified in a field **n2** characters wide.

Reference: 3.3

Colon Definition:
: .R

>R	Move the field width **n2** to the return stack.
S–>D	Convert **n1** to its double-precision equivalent.
R>	Move **n2** back to the parameter stack.
D.R	Output the value.
;	Terminate definition.

◇   ◇   ◇

/ (divide)   <f,s>

Stack: **n1 n2 > > > n3**

Leave the signed quotient **n3** of **n1** divided by **n2**. Any remainder will be dropped, with the integer result rounded towards zero.

Reference: 1.4.4, 2.1.1, 2.2

Colon Definition:
: /

/MOD	Leave the signed remainder and quotient.
SWAP DROP	Drop the remainder.
;	Terminate definition.

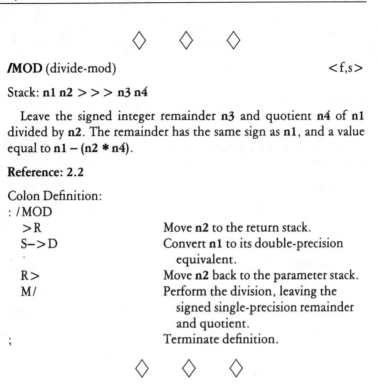

/MOD (divide-mod)   `<f,s>`

Stack: **n1 n2 > > > n3 n4**

Leave the signed integer remainder **n3** and quotient **n4** of **n1** divided by **n2**. The remainder has the same sign as **n1**, and a value equal to **n1 − (n2 * n4)**.

Reference: 2.2

Colon Definition:
: /MOD
   >R   Move **n2** to the return stack.
   S->D   Convert **n1** to its double-precision
                              equivalent.
   R>   Move **n2** back to the parameter stack.
   M/   Perform the division, leaving the
                              signed single-precision remainder
                              and quotient.
   ;   Terminate definition.

0 1 2 3   `<f>`

Stack: **> > > n**

System constants, to leave frequently-used small integers on the stack.

During execution, defined constants provide greater speed than conversion of input characters to numeric equivalents. When used as components in colon definitions, each of the defined constants will require only a 2-byte pointer rather than the four bytes needed for a compiled literal.

Reference: 3.2

0> (zero-less)   `<f,s>`

Stack: **n > > > f**

Leave a true flag if **n** is less than zero. Otherwise, leave a false flag.

Reference: 5.1

0= (zero-equals)   <f,s>

Stack: **n** > > > **f**

Leave a true flag if **n** equals zero. Otherwise, leave a false flag.
See **NOT**.

Reference: 5.1

0> (zero-greater)   <s>

Stack: **n** > > >**f**

Leave a true flag if **n** is greater than zero. Otherwise, leave a false
flag.

Reference: 5.1

0BRANCH   <f>

Stack: **f** > > >

Compiled by **IF**, **UNTIL**, and **WHILE** as the run-time procedure
for conditional branching.

When **IF**, **UNTIL**, or **WHILE** is encountered during compilation
of a colon-defined word <name>, the conditional is executed
immediately. In turn, it will compile a pointer to **0BRANCH** into
<name>'s parameter field. The cell immediately following will be
used to hold an in-line offset.

During later execution of <name>, **0BRANCH** tests the top
stack value as a flag. If the flag is true, execution of <name>
continues sequentially, using the pointer immediately after the
offset. If false, the compiled offset is used to transfer execution to the
designated location.

Reference: 5.5

◇   ◇   ◇

1+ (one-plus)   <f,s>

Stack: **n1 > > > n2**

Increment **n1** by one, leaving the result **n2**.

Reference: 2.2

Colon Definition:
: 1+
  1+   Add one to the top stack value.
;   Terminate definition.

◇   ◇   ◇

1− (one-minus)   <s>

Stack: **n1 > > > n2**

Decrement **n1** by one, leaving the result **n2**.

Reference: 2.2

◇   ◇   ◇

2! (two-store)   <z,x>

Stack: **d addr > > >**

Store the double-precision number **d** in the two cells (four bytes) beginning at **addr**. The high-order half of **d** will be stored in the lowest-numbered pair of bytes. The byte order within each half is installation-dependent.

Reference: 3.1

◇   ◇   ◇

2+ (two-plus)   <f,s>

Stack: **n1 > > > n2**

Increment **n1** by two, leaving the result **n2**.

Reference: 2.2

Colon Definition:
: 2+
  2 +   Add 2 to the top stack value.
;   Terminate definition.

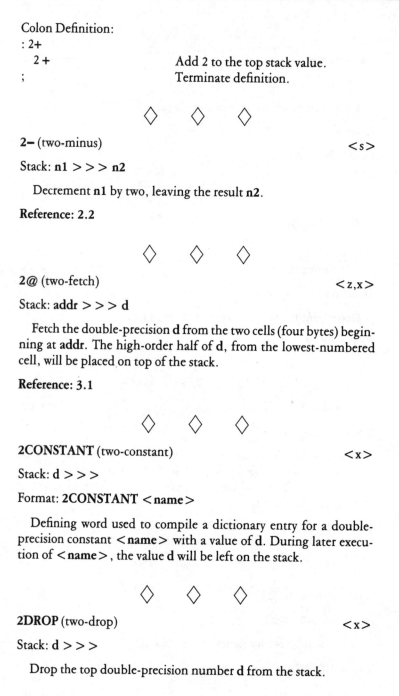

2– (two-minus)   <s>

Stack: **n1 > > > n2**

Decrement **n1** by two, leaving the result **n2**.

Reference: 2.2

2@ (two-fetch)   <z,x>

Stack: **addr > > > d**

Fetch the double-precision **d** from the two cells (four bytes) beginning at **addr**. The high-order half of **d**, from the lowest-numbered
cell, will be placed on top of the stack.

Reference: 3.1

2CONSTANT (two-constant)   <x>

Stack: **d > > >**

Format: **2CONSTANT** <name>

Defining word used to compile a dictionary entry for a double-
precision constant <name> with a value of **d**. During later execution of <name>, the value **d** will be left on the stack.

2DROP (two-drop)   <x>

Stack: **d > > >**

Drop the top double-precision number **d** from the stack.

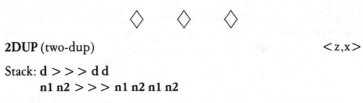

2DUP (two-dup)   < z,x >

Stack: **d** > > > **d d**
  n1 n2 > > > **n1 n2 n1 n2**

Duplicate the top double-precision number **d** or the top two single-precision values **n1** and **n2**. Equivalent to **OVER OVER**.

Reference: 2.3.4

2OVER (two-over)   < x >

Stack: **d1 d2** > > > **d1 d2 d1**

Leave a copy of the second double-precision number **d1** on top of the stack.

2ROT (two-rote)   < x >

Stack: **d1 d2 d3** > > > **d2 d3 d1**

Rotate the three top double-precision numbers, leaving the original third value **d1** on top of the stack.

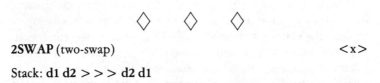

2SWAP (two-swap)   < x >

Stack: **d1 d2** > > > **d2 d1**

Exchange positions of the top two double-precision numbers on the stack.

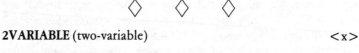

2VARIABLE (two-variable)   < x >

Format: **2VARIABLE** < name >

Defining word used to compile a dictionary definition for a double-precision variable <name>. The variable is not initialized. During later execution of <name>, the address of its parameter field containing the double-precision value will be placed on the stack.

79-STANDARD   <s>

Force an error condition if the core dictionary is not compatible with the FORTH-79 standard.

Reference: 4.3

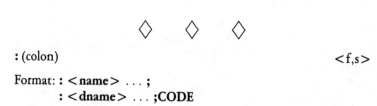

: (colon)   <f,s>

Format: : <name> ... ;
          : <dname> ... ;CODE

Defining word used to compile a dictionary definition for a word <name> or defining word <dname>.

Execution of : first causes the context vocabulary to be set to the current vocabulary. The stack pointer is saved for later error-checking. A header for <name> or <dname> is compiled beginning at the next available dictionary location; for fig-FORTH, the header's smudge bit is toggled. The link field contains a pointer to the name field of the next most recent addition to the current vocabulary.

Next, the value of user variable **STATE** is set to show compilation. Each non-immediate component word which follows in the input stream is compiled rather than executed; a pointer to each such word's code field is placed in the parameter field of the definition of <name> or <dname>. Literals are compiled as 16- or 32-bit binary values, with each 16 bits preceded by a pointer to the run-time procedure associated with **LITERAL**. Immediate words in the input stream are executed rather than compiled, regardless of the value of **STATE**. The compilation process terminates whenever either of the immediate words ; or ;CODE are executed.

During later execution of <name> or <dname>, the address interpreter will use the compiled pointers to sequentially execute the component words. By definition, the later execution of <name> or

<dname> is equivalent to execution of each of its components.

Fig-FORTH defines "colon" as an immediate word; FORTH-79 does not.

Reference: 1.1.3, 4.1, 4.2, 4.3, 7.2

; (semicolon) <f,s>

Format: : <name> ... ;

Immediate word to terminate compilation of a dictionary definition for <name> and return to the execution state.

When ; is encountered during compilation of <name>'s definition, it is executed immediately due to its precedence bit. After checking for a stack position error, it compiles a pointer to a run-time procedure as the final entry in <name>'s parameter field and sets the value of user variable **STATE** to zero. For fig-FORTH, <name>'s smudge bit is toggled back to zero.

During later execution of <name>, the run-time procedure will return control back to the text interpreter.

If compiling source code from mass storage, FORTH-79 and some versions of fig-FORTH require that the semicolon be located prior to exhaustion of the input stream containing the associated colon.

Reference: 1.1.3, 4.3, 5.5, 7.2.3, 12.4

Colon Definition:

: ;

?CSP	Issue an error message if the present stack pointer does not match the pointer stored in user variable **CSP**.
COMPILE ;S	Compile a pointer to the run-time routine in the next available location in <name>'s parameter field.
SMUDGE	Toggle the smudge bit back to zero.
[COMPILE] [	Suspend compilation and return to the execution state.
; IMMEDIATE	Terminate definition, set precedence.

;CODE (semicolon-code)   <f,x>

Format: **:** < dname > ... **;CODE mn**

Immediate word to terminate compilation of a new defining word
< dname >. Words later defined with < dname > will share the
generic execution procedure corresponding to the assembly mnemonics **mn**.

When **;CODE** is encountered during compilation of < dname >'s
definition, it is executed immediately due to its precedence bit.
After checking for a stack position error, a pointer to the run-time
routine is compiled in < dname >'s parameter field. The context
vocabulary is set to **ASSEMBLER** and the value of user variable
STATE is set for execution. Execution of the **ASSEMBLER** words
designated by **mn** compile the machine code generic execution
procedure at the end of < dname >'s parameter field.

During later execution of < dname >, in the form

< dname > < name >

a new header is created for < name >. The run-time procedure
compiled by **;CODE** executes by modifying < name >'s code field
contents to point to the generic execution procedure, then returns
control to the interpreter.

If compiling source code from mass storage, FORTH-79 and some
versions of fig-FORTH require that **;CODE** be located prior to
exhaustion of the input stream containing the associated colon.

Reference: 8.3, 12.4

Colon Definition:
: ;CODE

?CSP	Issue an error message if the present stack pointer differs from the value saved in user variable **CSP**.
COMPILE (;CODE)	Compile a pointer to the run-time procedure in the next available location in < dname >'s parameter field.
[COMPILE] [	Suspend compilation and return to the execution state.
[COMPILE] ASSEMBLER	Set the context vocabulary to assemble the following assembly

mnemonics (note that **[COMPILE]** is not shown in the model's definition, but is required to compile the immediate **ASSEMBLER** word).

SMUDGE	Toggle the smudge bit back to zero.
; IMMEDIATE	Terminate definition, set precedence.

;S (stop)   <f>

Immediate word compiled by **;** as the run-time procedure to return control to the interpreter at the end of execution of a colon-defined word. Also used to stop interpretation of a source code screen.

When **;** is encountered during compilation of a colon-defined word, it is executed immediately due to its precedence bit. In turn, it compiles a pointer to **;S** as the final component of the definition under construction. During later execution of that definition, **;S** will use the top value from the return stack to return to the calling definition.

When encountered during loading of a source code screen from disk, **;S** halts loading. Any further contents of the screen are ignored, and control returns to the calling definition.

Reference: 5.5, 7.2.3, 11.4

< (less-than)   <f,s>

Stack: **n1 n2 > > > f**

Leave a true flag if the signed value **n1** is less than **n2**. Otherwise, leave a false flag.

Reference: 5.1

Colon Definition:

: **<**	
—	Compare **n1** and **n2** by subtraction.
0**<**	True if **n1** was less than **n2**.
;	Terminate definition.

< # (less-sharp)   **<f,s>**

Format: **< # ... # >**

Begin conversion of an unsigned double-precision number into a pictured output text string. For fig-FORTH, the string will be created in reverse order, immediately below the text buffer; FORTH-79 does not explicitly state a location.

Reference: 9.5

Colon Definition:
: <#

    PAD   Leave a pointer to the text buffer.

    HLD !   Initialize a pointer to the last
                                 character.

;   Terminate definition.

< BUILDS (builds)   **<f>**

Format: **:** < dname> **< BUILDS ... DOES >** ... **;**

Defining word used to specify the compilation behavior of a class of words compiled by < dname>.

During later execution of < dname>, in the form
                    < dname> < name>

< BUILDS compiles an unsmudged header for a new word < name>, and a parameter field with a dummy zero value. Any words which follow, up to **DOES >** , may execute to modify or extend the new definition. Execution of **DOES >** modifies the code field of < name> and replaces the dummy parameter with a pointer to the generic execution procedure specified by the words following **DOES >** .

When < name> is later executed, the address of its first usable parameter field location (beyond the pointer in the first cell) will initially be left on the stack. Subsequent execution of < name> is in accordance with the generic execution procedure shared by all words compiled using < dname>.

Reference: 8.4

Colon Definition:
: < BUILDS
   0 CONSTANT   Compile a new header for the next
                             word < **name** > in the input
                             stream, with a zero value in the
                             parameter field and a code field
                             pointing to the generic procedure
                             of **CONSTANT**.
;   Terminate definition.

= (equals)   < f,s >

Stack: **n1 n2** > > > **f**

    Leave a true flag if **n1** and **n2** are equal. Otherwise, leave a false
flag.

Reference: 5.1

Colon Definition:
: =
     −   Subtract **n1** from **n2**.
    0=   Leave a true flag if the subtraction
                             result was zero; otherwise, leave a
                             false flag.
;   Terminate definition.

> (greater-than)   < f,s >

Stack: **n1 n2** > > > **f**

    Leave a true flag if the signed value **n1** is greater than **n2**. Other-
wise, leave a false flag.

Reference: 5.1

Colon Definition:
: >
   SWAP   Exchange positions of **n1** and **n2**.
     <   Leave a true flag if **n2** is less than **n1**;
                             otherwise, leave a false flag.
;   Terminate definition.

>IN (to-in)   `<s>`

Stack: **> > > addr**

   User variable containing an offset pointer corresponding to the
next character in the input stream. At execution, the location of the
pointer within the user area will be left on the stack.
   See **IN**.

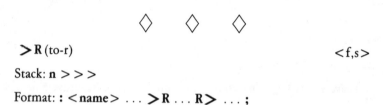

>R (to-r)   `<f,s>`

Stack: **n > > >**

Format: **: <name> ... >R ... R> ... ;**

   Move the top single-precision value from the parameter stack to
the return stack.
   The value must be removed from the return stack within the same
colon definition. If used within a compilation structure such as a
nested loop or conditional, both **>R** and **R>** must appear within
the same nesting level.

Reference: 6.8, 12.1

? (question-mark)   `<f,s>`

Stack: **addr > > >**

   Output the signed single-precision value stored in the cell (two
bytes) beginning at **addr**, followed by one space.

Reference: 3.1

Colon Definition:
: ?
    @   Fetch the stored value.
    .   Output the value in signed form,
                                    followed by a space.
    ;   Terminate definition.

◇   ◇   ◇

?COMP (query-compiling)   <f>

Issue an error message if not compiling.

Reference: B.1

Colon Definition:
: ?COMP
  STATE @   Fetch the compilation state flag.
  0=   Leave a true flag if not compiling.
  17 ?ERROR   If true, issue error message 17.
;   Terminate definition.

◇   ◇   ◇

?CSP (query-c-s-p)   <f>

Issue an error message if the current stack pointer does not match the pointer saved in user variable **CSP**.

Reference: B.1

Colon Definition:
: ?CSP
  SP@ CSP @   Fetch the two pointers.
  −   Compare the values by subtraction.
  20 ?ERROR   If not equal, issue error message 20.
;   Terminate definition.

◇   ◇   ◇

?DUP (query-dup)   <s>

Stack: **n > > > n**   (n equals zero)
    n > > > n n   (non-zero n)

Leave two copies of the top stack value **n** if **n** is non-zero, or only one if **n** equals zero.
  See **−DUP**.

Reference: 1.4

◇   ◇   ◇

?ERROR (query-error)   <f>

Stack: **f n** > > >

If flag **f** is true, perform the error notification and recovery routine
for error number **n**.

Colon Definition:
: ?ERROR
  SWAP   Exchange **f** and **n** on stack.
  IF   True branch — error detected.
    ERROR   Perform the error notification and
         recovery routine for error number
         n, in accordance with the value of
         WARNING.
  ELSE   False branch — no error.
   DROP   Drop **n** from the stack.
  ENDIF   Terminate conditional.
;   Terminate definition.

◇   ◇   ◇

?EXEC (query-exec)   <f>

Issue an error message if not executing.

Reference: B.1

Colon Definition:
: ?EXEC
  STATE @   Fetch the compilation state flag.
  18 ?ERROR   If non-zero (compiling), issue error
         message 18.
;   Terminate definition.

◇   ◇   ◇

?LOADING (query-loading)   <f>

Issue an error message if not loading and interpreting source code
from an editing screen.

Reference: B.1

Colon Definition:
: ?LOADING

   BLK@   Fetch the number of the block
                                         currently being interpreted. A zero
                                         denotes terminal input.

   0=   Leave a true flag if input is from the
                                         terminal.

   22 ?ERROR   If input is from the terminal, issue
                                         error message 22.

;   Terminate definition.

◇   ◇   ◇

?PAIRS (query-pairs)   <f>

Stack: **n1 n2 > > >**

Issue an error message if **n1** and **n2** are not equal.

Reference: B.1

Colon Definition:
: ?PAIRS

   −   Subtract **n2** from **n1**, and leave the
                                         result as a flag.

   19 ?ERROR   If not equal, issue error message 19.

;   Terminate definition.

◇   ◇   ◇

?STACK (query-stack)   <f>

Issue an error message if the parameter stack is out of bounds.
The model definition of ?STACK is installation-dependent, with
stack boundaries specified as literals. The following definition is
found in the fig-FORTH 8080/Z-80 core.

Reference: B.1

Colon Definition:
: ?STACK   NOTE: 8080/Z-80 definition.

   SP@ S0 @   Fetch the current and initial stack
                                         pointer values.

   SWAP   Exchange the pointer positions.

U<	Leave a true flag if the stack has underflowed.
1 ?ERROR	If underflow exists, issue error message 1.
SP@	Fetch the current stack pointer again.
HERE 80 +	Leave a pointer to the first byte above the output buffer.
U<	Leave a true flag if the stack has overflowed.
7 ?ERROR	If overflow exists, issue error message 7.
;	Terminate definition.

?TERMINAL (query-terminal)   <f>

Stack: > > > f

Installation-dependent routine to check the terminal input for a "break" keypress. If found, a true flag will be left on the stack. Otherwise, a false flag will be left.

Reference: 9.1

@ (fetch)   <f,s>

Stack: **addr** > > > **n**

Leave the single-precision value **n** stored in the cell (two bytes) beginning at **addr**.

Reference: 3.1

◇   ◇   ◇

ABORT   <f,s>

Warm start procedure to clear both the parameter stack and the return stack, and enter the execution state. The dictionary pointer and contents are not changed. After an installation-dependent message has been output, control returns to the terminal for further input.

Reference: 12.3

Colon Definition:
: ABORT

SP!	Reinitialize the parameter stack pointer.
DECIMAL	Set the input/output base for decimal.
DR0	Select drive 0 as the current disk.
CR . "xxx"	Output an installation-dependent message.
[COMPILE] FORTH	Set the context vocabulary to **FORTH**.
DEFINITIONS	Set the current vocabulary to **FORTH**.
QUIT	Restart the interpreter loop.
;	Terminate definition.

ABS (absolute)   <f,s>

Stack: **n > > > u**

Leave the absolute value **u** of the signed single-precision number **n**.

Reference: 2.2

Colon Definition:
: ABS

DUP	Copy **n**.
+ –	Leave **u**, with the magnitude of **n** and a positive sign.
;	Terminate definition.

AGAIN   <f>

Stack: **addr n > > >**   (compilation)

Format: **: < name >** ... **BEGIN** ... **AGAIN** ... **;**

Immediate word to complete compilation of an indefinite loop which does not contain a test for execution completion.

When encountered during compilation of < **name** >'s dictionary definition, **AGAIN** executes immediately due to its precedence bit. In turn, a pointer to the run-time unconditional branching routine is compiled into < **name** >'s parameter field. The pointer is followed by an in-line offset, calculated using the **addr** operand left by **BEGIN**. The value **n**, also left by **BEGIN**, is used for error checking.

During later execution of < **name** >, the offset is used to transfer execution back to the first word of the loop. The loop will continue until **ABORT** or **COLD**, or until the sequence **R> DROP** is executed one level below.

Reference: 5.4, 12.4

Colon Definition:
: AGAIN

1 ?PAIRS	Test the error check value **n**. If not equal to 1, issue an error message.
COMPILE BRANCH	Compile a pointer to the run-time routine in the next available location in < **name** >'s parameter field.
BACK	Use **addr** to calculate and compile the backward offset to the top of the loop.
; IMMEDIATE	Terminate definition, set precedence.

◇   ◇   ◇

ALLOT   < f,s >

Stack: **n** > > >

Increment the current dictionary pointer by **n**. The operand **n** specifies a number of bytes, except for fig-FORTH systems with processors using cell addressing rather than byte addressing.

Reference: 6.3, 6.6, 7.2, 7.3, B.1

Colon Definition:
: ALLOT

DP	Leave the address containing the current dictionary pointer value.
+!	Increment the contents by **n**.
;	Terminate definition.

AND <f,s>

Stack: **n1 n2 > > > n3**

Leave the bit-by-bit logical "and" **n3** of **n1** and **n2**. The i-th bit of **n3** is set to 1 if and only if the i-th bits of **n1** and **n2** are both 1.

Reference: 2.5, 3.3.6

ASSEMBLER <x>

Immediate vocabulary defining word to select the **ASSEMBLER** vocabulary as the context vocabulary for dictionary searches.

Reference: 7.1, 8.2, 8.3

B/BUF (b-buf) <f>

Stack: **> > > n**

System constant to leave the number of data bytes per disk block on the stack. The value of **B/BUF** must be a power of two, and cannot exceed 1024. FORTH-79 presumes that all blocks contain 1024 data bytes.

Reference: 6.10, 10.1, 10.2

B/SCR (b-screen) <f>

Stack: **> > > n**

System constant to leave the number of disk blocks per source code editing screen. Each screen contains 1024 data bytes, which may be visualized as 16 lines of 64 characters.

Reference: 11.2

BACK   \<f\>

Stack: **addr > > >**

Calculate the offset from the present top of the dictionary back to
addr, and compile it into the next dictionary location.

Colon Definition:
: BACK
   HERE   Fetch the current dictionary pointer.
     – ,   Calculate and compile the offset.
 ;   Terminate definition.

BASE   \<f,s\>

Stack: **> > > addr**

User variable containing the current numeric input/output base.
All I/O values are converted to internal binary representation in
accordance with the base value. At execution, the location of the
value within the user area will be left on the stack.

Reference: 3.3, 4.3, 6.9, 12.2

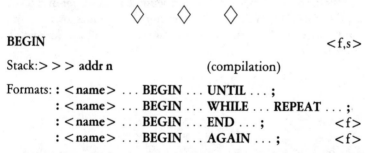

BEGIN   \<f,s\>

Stack:**> > > addr n**   (compilation)

Formats: : \<name\> ... **BEGIN** ... **UNTIL** ... ;
       : \<name\> ... **BEGIN** ... **WHILE** ... **REPEAT** ... ;
       : \<name\> ... **BEGIN** ... **END** ... ;   \<f\>
       : \<name\> ... **BEGIN** ... **AGAIN** ... ;   \<f\>

Immediate word to begin compilation of an indefinite loop.

During compilation of \<name\>'s dictionary definition, **BEGIN**
executes immediately due to its precedence bit. The current dictionary pointer **addr** is left on the stack, along with an error check
value **n**. The **addr** result will later be used to compile an offset back
to the top of the loop.

During execution, **UNTIL** or **END** cause repetition of the loop if the top stack value at that time is a false flag. If a true flag is found, execution continues with the next word following the loop.

The top stack value will be tested within the loop by **WHILE**. If the flag at that time is true, the words between **WHILE** and **REPEAT** will be executed and the loop restarted; if false, the words between **WHILE** and **REPEAT** are ignored and execution continues after the loop.

AGAIN unconditionally repeats the entire loop.

Reference: 5.4, 5.5, 12.4

Colon Definition:
: BEGIN
    ?COMP   Issue an error message if not
                                 compiling.
    HERE 1   Leave the current dictionary pointer
                                 and an error check value.
; IMMEDIATE   Terminate definition, set precedence.

◇   ◇   ◇

BL (blank)   <f>

Stack: > > > **n**

System constant to leave the ASCII code of a "blank" character on the stack.

◇   ◇   ◇

BLANKS   <f>

Stack: **addr n** > > >

Place a "blank" character (ASCII code 32) in **n** consecutive memory bytes, beginning at **addr**.

In some versions of fig-FORTH, **BLANKS** will not store any characters if **n** is not greater than zero.

Reference: 3.1

Colon Definition:
; BLANKS
    BL   Leave the ASCII code for "blank" on
                                 the stack.

FILL   Fill **n** bytes with "blank" characters.
;   Terminate definition.

BLK (b-l-k)   <f,s>

Stack: > > > **addr**

User variable containing the number of the disk block currently being interpreted. A value of zero denotes input from the terminal rather than disk. At execution, the location of the value within the user area will be left on the stack.

Reference: 11.1, 12.2

BLOCK   <f,s>

Stack: **n** > > > **addr**

Leave the address of the first data byte of the block buffer containing disk block **n**. If not already in memory, block **n** is read into a mass storage buffer; if the buffer's update bit was set, the prior contents of that buffer are first written back to the disk.

The operand **n** is specified relative to the start of the current drive in fig-FORTH; FORTH-79 block numbers are always absolute offsets. Only the addresses of data within the block most recently referenced by **BLOCK** are assured of validity.

Reference: 10.3, 11.2

Colon Definition:
: BLOCK
  OFFSET @ +   Leave the absolute block number.
  >R   Save the result on the return stack.
  PREV @ DUP   Fetch and copy the header address of
                                    the most recently referenced buffer.
  @   Fetch the block number from the
                                      header.
  R −   Compare with the designated block.
  DUP +   Discard the most significant (update)
                                      bit from the comparison result.

IF	Outer true branch — block **n** not most recent.
BEGIN	Begin a conditional loop.
+BUF	Advance the buffer header address. Leave a true flag if **PREV** does not point to the buffer; otherwise, leave a false flag.
0=	Reverse the flag.
IF	Inner true branch — all buffers have been checked.
DROP	Drop the buffer header address.
R	Copy the desired block number from the return stack.
BUFFER	Assign the next buffer to the block. If the update bit of the buffer is set, write the contents back to the disk. Leave the address of the first data byte of the buffer.
DUP	Duplicate the data address.
R	Copy the desired block number again.
1 R/W	Read the block from the disk.
2 −	Decrement the address to point to the buffer's header.
ENDIF	Terminate inner conditional.
DUP @	Duplicate the buffer header address.
R − DUP +	Compare the header's block number with the desired one. A non-zero result denotes no match.
0=	Reverse the flag.
UNTIL	Repeat the loop until a match is found or all buffers have been checked, and the desired block has been located or input.
DUP PREV !	Copy and save the latest buffer header address.
ENDIF	Terminate outer conditional.
R > DROP	Remove the desired block number from the return stack.
2+	Increment the header address to point to the first data byte in the buffer.
;	Terminate definition.

BLOCK-READ   <f>

Installation-dependent routine to transmit one block of data from the disk to a mass storage buffer.

BLOCK-WRITE   <f>

Installation-dependent routine to transmit one block of data from a mass storage buffer to the disk.

BRANCH   <f>

Compiled by **ELSE**, **REPEAT**, and **AGAIN** as the run-time procedure for unconditional branching.

When one of the listed conditionals is encountered during compilation of colon-defined word <**name**>, it is executed immediately. In turn, it will compile a pointer to **BRANCH** into <**name**>'s parameter field. The cell immediately following will be used to hold an in-line offset.

During later execution of <**name**>, **BRANCH** transfers execution to the designated location.

Reference: 5.5

BUFFER   <f,s>

Stack: **n > > > addr**

Assign the disk buffer whose first data byte is at **addr** to block **n**, without reading it from the disk. The current contents of the buffer will be written back to the disk if the buffer's update bit is set.

The operand **n** is specified as an absolute offset from the start of drive 0.

Reference: 10.3

Colon Definition:
: BUFFER

USE @	Leave a pointer to the header of the buffer least recently used.
DUP >R	Save one copy of the address on the return stack.
BEGIN	Begin an indefinite loop.
+BUF	Advance the buffer address. Leave a true flag if **PREV** does not point to the buffer; otherwise, leave a false flag.
UNTIL	Repeat loop to skip the buffer pointed to by **PREV**.
USE !	Update the pointer for use on the next access.
R	Copy the address of the buffer to be used.
@ 0<	Fetch the buffer header contents. Leave a true flag if the most significant (update) bit is set to 1.
IF	True branch — update bit set.
R 2+	Leave a pointer to the first data byte.
R @	Fetch the current header bytes.
32767 AND	Mask the update bit (using 7FFFH), leaving the block number.
0 R/W	Write the buffer's contents to the disk.
ENDIF	Terminate conditional.
R !	Store the block number in the buffer header.
R PREV !	Save a pointer to the most recently assigned buffer.
R>	Remove the buffer address from the return stack.
2+	Increment the address to point to the first data byte.
;	Terminate definition.

◇   ◇   ◇

C! (c-store)   <f,s>

Stack: **b addr** > > >

Store byte **b** at location **addr**.

Reference: 3.1

◇   ◇   ◇

C, (c-comma)   <f,s>

Stack: **b** > > >

Store byte **b** in the next available byte in the dictionary at the location pointed to by the dictionary pointer. The pointer is then incremented to point to the next available location.

Reference: 7.3

Colon Definition:
: C,

HERE	Leave a pointer to the next available dictionary location.
C!	Store byte **b**.
1 ALLOT	Increment the dictionary pointer.
;	Terminate definition.

◇   ◇   ◇

C/L (c-l)   <f>

Stack: > > > **n**

System constant to leave the number of characters per source code editing screen line.

Note that **C/L** is not listed in the standard fig-FORTH glossary, but is defined in the model.

Reference: 9.1

◇   ◇   ◇

C@ (c-fetch)   <f,s>

Stack: **addr** > > > **b**

Leave the byte contents **b** of the location **addr** on the stack, padded with zeros to fill the stack location.

Reference: 3.1

CFA (c-f-a)   <f>

Stack: **addr1** > > > **addr2**

Leave the code field address **addr2** of the definition whose parameter field starts at **addr1**.

Reference: 7.2

Colon Definition:
: CFA
   2 –   Decrement the parameter field
                              address.
   ;   Terminate definition.

CMOVE (c-move)   <f,s>

Stack: **addr1 addr2 n** > > >

Move **n** bytes, beginning at **addr1**, to the memory locations beginning at **addr2**. The move proceeds from low to high memory.

For FORTH-79 and some versions of fig-FORTH, **CMOVE** will not move any bytes if **n** is not greater than zero.

Reference: 3.1

CODE   <x>

Format: **CODE** < name > mn **END-CODE**

Defining word used to compile a header for < name > and the machine code corresponding to the assembly mnemonics **mn**. The code field of < name > will contain a pointer to its parameter field. **ASSEMBLER** becomes the context vocabulary.

Reference: 8.2

COLD   <f>

Cold start procedure to reset all pointers, stacks, and user variables to their initialization values. All further I/O is via the terminal, with the text interpreter loop restarted in the execution mode. Any user-defined dictionary definitions are lost.

Reference: 4.1, 6.2, 6.3, 12.3

COMPILE   <f,s>

Format: **:** < name > ... **COMPILE** < name1 > ... **;**

Compile a pointer to < name1 > at the current top of the diction-ary during run-time. Each time < name > is executed, the code field address of < name1 > will be placed into the next dictionary location.

Reference: 5.5

Colon Definition:
: COMPILE

?COMP	Issue an error message if not compiling.
R>	Move the pointer to the next word < name1 > in the input stream.
DUP 2+	Duplicate the pointer, incrementing one copy to point to the next word after < name1 > in the input stream.
>R	Move the incremented pointer back to the return stack.
@ ,	Fetch the code field address of < name1 > and compile it into the top of the dictionary.
;	Terminate definition.

CONSTANT   <f,s>

Stack: **n** > > >

Format: **CONSTANT** < name >

Defining word used to create a dictionary entry for < name > containing the constant value **n** in its parameter field. When < name > is later executed, its value **n** will be left on the stack.

Reference: 3.2, 4.1, 4.2, 7.2, 8.3

Colon Definition:
: CONSTANT

CREATE	Create a dictionary header for the next word < name > taken from the input stream, and a code field pointing to the parameter field.
SMUDGE	Unsmudge the header's smudge bit.
,	Compile **n** into the first location of < name >'s parameter field.
;CODE mn	Terminate compilation of **CONSTANT** by compiling a pointer to the associated run-time procedure and the machine code corresponding to mnemonics **mn**. When **CONSTANT** is later executed, the code field of < name > will be changed to point to the generic procedure specified by **mn**.

CONTEXT   <f,s>

Stack: > > > **addr**

User variable containing a pointer to a parameter in the vocabulary defining word specifying the context vocabulary; that location in turn contains a pointer to the name field of the most recent addition to that vocabulary. Dictionary searches will begin in the context vocabulary; fig-FORTH will also search the current vocabulary as well. At execution, the location of the pointer within the user area will be left on the stack.

Reference: 6.9, 7.4

CONVERT   <s>

Stack: **d1 addr1 > > > d2 addr2**

Convert a dimensioned text string beginning at **addr1** into its numeric equivalent, using the current number base. Double-precision number **d1** serves as an accumulator, with the result being left as **d2**. A pointer **addr2** to the first unconvertible character is left on top of the stack.
See **(NUMBER)**.

Reference: 9.5

COUNT   <f,s>

Stack: **addr1 > > > addr2 n**

For a dimensioned text string with a count byte at **addr1**, leave the location **addr2** of the first text character and the count **n** on the stack.

Reference: 9.2, 9.3

Colon Definition:
: COUNT
   DUP   Copy the count byte address.
   1+ SWAP   Increment one copy to **addr2**, and
                                    exchange positions.
   C@   Fetch the contents **n** of the length
                                    byte at **addr1**.
;   Terminate definition.

CR (c-r)   \<f,s\>

Installation-dependent routine to send the ASCII codes for a carriage return and line feed to the terminal.

Reference: 1.1.1, 3.3, 9.1, 9.3

CREATE   \<f,s\>

Format: **CREATE** \<name\>

Create a dictionary header for \<name\>, beginning at the next available dictionary location. No parameter field space is allocated.

For fig-FORTH, the code field of \<name\> contains a pointer to its parameter field, for use with a primitive definition. For FORTH-79, the code field contents will be identical to a variable. In either event, the definition is linked to the current vocabulary.

Reference: 8.1, 8.2, 8.3, 8.4, B.1

Colon Definition:
: CREATE

−FIND	Copy the next blank-delimited word from the input stream to the word buffer, and search for a match. If found, the word's parameter field address and length byte are left on the stack, below a true flag; otherwise, only a false flag is left.
IF	True branch — match found.
DROP	Drop the length byte.
NFA ID.	Output the matching word's name.
4 MESSAGE SPACE	Output warning message 4.
ENDIF	Terminate conditional.
HERE DUP C@	Leave the address and contents of the input word's length byte.
WIDTH @ MIN	Set the length to the minimum of the length or name-length limit.
1+ ALLOT	Set the dicionary pointer to the next byte after the name.

DUP	Duplicate the name field pointer.
160 TOGGLE	Toggle the high bit and the smudge bit of the length byte, using the constant (0A0H).
HERE 1 −	Leave a pointer to the last stored name character.
128 TOGGLE	Toggle the high bit of the final stored character, using the constant (80H).
LATEST	Leave a pointer to the name field of the most recent addition to the current vocabulary.
,	Compile the pointer into <**name**>'s link field.
CURRENT @	Fetch the pointer to the vocabulary defining word of the current vocabulary.
!	Store <**name**>'s name field address in the parameter field of the current vocabulary's defining word.
HERE 2+ ,	Compile a code field pointing to the parameter field of <**name**>.
;	Terminate definition.

◇   ◇   ◇

CSP (c-s-p)   <f>

Stack: > > > **addr**

   User variable containing a temporary pointer to the top of the parameter stack. At execution, the location of the pointer within the user area will be left on the stack.

Reference: 12.4

◇   ◇   ◇

CURRENT   <f,s>

Stack: > > > **addr**

   User variable containing a pointer to the parameter in the vocabulary defining word specifying the current vocabulary; that location in turn contains a pointer to the name field of the most recent addition to that vocabulary. New definitions will be linked to the current vocabulary. Fig-FORTH will also search the current vocabulary after the context vocabulary has been exhausted. At execution, the location of the pointer within the user area will be left on the stack.

Reference: 6.9, 7.4

D+ (d-plus)   <f,s>

Stack: **d1 d2 > > > d3**

Leave the signed sum **d3** of double-precision numbers **d1** and **d2**.

Reference: 2.3

D+− (d-plus-minus)   <f>

Stack: **d1 n > > > d2**

Leave **d2**, with the magnitude of **d1** and the sign of **n∗d1**.

Reference: 2.3

Colon Definition:
: D+−
   0<   Leave a true flag if **n** is negative.
   IF DMINUS ENDIF   Negate **d1** if **n** is negative.
;   Terminate definition.

D− (d-minus)   <x>

Stack: **d1 d2 > > > d3**

Subtract **d2** from **d1**, and leave the signed result **d3** on top of the stack.

D. (d-dot)   <f,x>

Stack: **d** > > >

Output a signed double-precision value **d** followed by one space to the terminal. A preceding negative sign will be printed if the most significant bit of **d** is set to 1.

Reference: 2.3, 3.3

Colon Definition:
: D.
0	Leave a dummy field width.
D.R	Output the number, with no leading blanks.
SPACE	Output a trailing blank.
;	Terminate definition.

D.R (d-dot-r)   <f,x>

Stack: **d n** > > >

Output the value **d** right-justified in a field **n** characters wide to the terminal.

Reference: 3.3

Colon Definition:
: D.R
>R	Move the field width **n** to the return stack.
SWAP OVER	Leave an extra copy of the high-order half of **d** beneath **d** on the stack.
DABS	Convert **d** to its absolute value.
< # #S SIGN #>	Convert the value to a pictured output string. Leave the address of the leftmost character and the length byte on the stack.
R>	Move the field width back to the parameter stack.

OVER –	Subtract the length from the field width.
SPACES	Output leftmost padding blanks.
TYPE	Output the string.
;	Terminate definition.

◇   ◇   ◇

D0= (d-zero-equals)   <x>

Stack: **d** > > > **f**

Leave a true flag if the double-precision number **d** equals zero. Otherwise, leave a false flag.

◇   ◇   ◇

D< (d-less-than)   <s,x>

Stack: **d1 d2** > > > **f**

Leave a true flag if the signed double-precision **d1** is less than **d2**. Otherwise, leave a false flag.

Reference: 5.1

◇   ◇   ◇

D= (d-equals)   <x>

Stack: **d1 d2** > > > **f**

Leave a true flag if the signed double-precision numbers **d1** and **d2** are equal. Otherwise, leave a false flag.

◇   ◇   ◇

DABS (d-absolute)   <f,x>

Stack: **d** > > > **ud**

Leave the absolute value **ud** of the signed double-precision number **d**.

Reference: 2.3

Colon Definition:
: DABS
   DUP   Copy the high-order half of **d**.
   D+−   Leave **ud** with the magnitude of **d** and
                    a positive sign.
;   Terminate definition.

◇   ◇   ◇

DECIMAL   <f,s>

Set the base for numeric input/output to decimal.

Reference: 3.3, 4.3.2, 4.3.5

Colon Definition:
: DECIMAL
   10 BASE !   Store decimal 10 in the user variable
                    BASE.
;   Terminate definition.

◇   ◇   ◇

DEFINITIONS   <f,s>

Set the current vocabulary to the context vocabulary. New word definitions will be linked to the current vocabulary.

Reference: 7.1

Colon Definition:
: DEFINITIONS
   CONTEXT @   Fetch the pointer to the vocabulary
                    defining word specifying the
                    context vocabulary.
   CURRENT !   Store the same pointer for the current
                    vocabulary.
;   Terminate definition.

◇   ◇   ◇

DENSITY   <z>

Stack: > > > **addr**

System variable containing a disk density flag. A value of 0 denotes single density; a value of 1 indicates double density. At execution, the address of the variable's parameter field is placed on the stack.

DEPTH <s>

Stack: > > > **n**

Leave the number **n** of 16-bit stack locations in use immediately before **DEPTH** was executed.

Reference: 1.4, 4.3.6

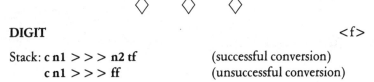

DIGIT <f>

Stack: **c n1** > > > **n2 tf** (successful conversion)
      c n1 > > > **ff** (unsuccessful conversion)

If possible, convert an ASCII character **c** to its binary equivalent **n2** in accordance with the current I/O base **n1** and leave a true flag. If **c** does not correspond to a valid digit, leave only a false flag.

DISK-ERROR <z>

Stack: > > > **addr**

System variable containing a disk status flag. A non-zero value indicates that an error occurred in reading or writing the last sector.

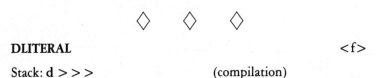

DLITERAL <f>

Stack: **d** > > > (compilation)

Immediate word used by the text interpreter to compile a double-precision value as an in-line literal.

During compilation of a colon definition, each half of the double-precision number **d** is separately compiled as a literal preceded by a pointer to the associated run-time routine. During later execution of the definition, each half of the literal value will be placed on the stack.

DLITERAL has no effect during execution.

Reference: 5.5

Colon Definition:
: DLITERAL

STATE @	Fetch the user variable **STATE** containing the compilation state.
IF	True branch — compilation state.
SWAP	Exchange the positions of the high- and low-order halves of **d** on the stack.
[COMPILE] LITERAL	Compile the low-order half, along with a pointer to the run-time routine.
[COMPILE] LITERAL	Compile the high-order half, along with a pointer to the run-time routine.
ENDIF	Terminate conditional.
; IMMEDIATE	Terminate definition, set precedence.

◇   ◇   ◇

DMAX (d-max)   <x>

Stack: **d1 d2 > > > d3**

Leave the maximum **d3** of the signed double-precision numbers **d1** and **d2**.

DMIN (d-min)   <x>

Stack: **d1 d2 7 > > d3**

Leave the minimum **d3** of the signed double-precision numbers **d1** and **d2**.

DMIN (d-min)   <x>

Stack: **d1 d2 > > > d3**

Leave the minimum **d3** of the signed double-precision numbers **d1** and **d2**.
See **DNEGATE**.

Reference: 2.3

DNEGATE (d-negate)   <s>

Stack: **d1 > > > d2**

Leave the two's complement of the double-precision number **d2**, with the same magnitude but opposite sign of **d1**.
See **DMINUS**.

Reference: 2.3

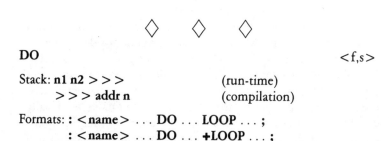

DO   <f,s>

Stack: **n1 n2 > > >**   (run-time)
     > > > addr n   (compilation)

Formats: **: <name> ... DO ... LOOP ... ;**
       : <name> ... DO ... +LOOP ... ;

Immediate word to begin compilation of an indexed loop.

During compilation of **<name>**'s dictionary definition, **DO** executes immediately due to its precedence bit. In turn, a pointer to the run-time routine is compiled into **<name>**'s parameter field. The current dictionary pointer **addr** and an error check value **n** are left on the stack. The address will later be used to compile an offset back to the top of the loop.

During later execution of **<name>**, the run-time routine will move the loop limit **n1** and initial index **n2** to the return stack.

Reference: 5.3, 5.5, 12.4

Colon Definition:
: DO
    COMPILE (DO)   Compile a pointer to the run-time
                                routine in the next available
                                dictionary location.
      HERE 3   Leave the current dictionary pointer
                                and an error check value.
    ; IMMEDIATE   Terminate definition, set precedence.

$$\diamond \qquad \diamond \qquad \diamond$$

DOES> (does)   <f,s>

Formats: : <dname> **<BUILDS . . . DOES>** . . . ;   <f>
        : <dname> **CREATE . . . DOES>** . . . ;   <s>

Defining word used to specify the generic execution behavior of a class of words compiled by <dname>. Significant differences exist between the fig-FORTH and FORTH-79 versions.

For fig-FORTH, **DOES>** is compiled as a component in the normal manner during compilation of <dname>'s dictionary entry. During later execution of <dname>, in the form
                <dname> <name>
<BUILDS compiles a definition for <name> with a dummy zero parameter. Any words which follow in <dname>'s definition, up to **DOES>** , may execute to modify or extend the new definition. **DOES>** executes by modifying the code field of <name>, and replacing the dummy parameter with a pointer to the generic execution procedure specified by the words following **DOES>** . Finally, during later execution of <name>, the address of its first usable parameter field location (beyond the pointer in the first cell) will initially be left on the stack. Subsequent execution of <name> is in accordance with the generic execution procedure specified by <dname>.

For FORTH-79, **DOES>** is an immediate word which executes during compilation of <dname>'s dictionary definition. A pointer to a run-time routine is compiled into <dname>'s parameter field, along with a machine code routine specifying the generic execution behavior of all high-level defining words. During later execution of <dname>, in the form
                <dname> <name>
CREATE compiles a header for <name>. Any words which follow

in <dname>'s definition, up to **DOES>** , may execute to modify or extend the new definition. The run-time procedure associated with **DOES>** rewrites the code field contents of <name> to point to the generic execution procedure. Finally, during later execution of <name>, the address of its first parameter field location will initially be left on the stack. Subsequent execution of <name> is in accordance with the generic execution procedure specified by <dname>.

Reference: 8.4

Colon Definition:
: DOES>

R>	Fetch the pointer to the next word after **DOES>** in the input stream.
LATEST PFA	Fetch a pointer to <name>'s first parameter location.
!	Replace the dummy parameter with a pointer to the next word following **DOES>** .
;CODE mn	Terminate definition of **DOES>** by compiling a pointer to the run-time routine into the parameter field of **DOES>** , along with the machine code corresponding to the assembler mnemonics **mn**. During later execution of **DOES>** , the code field of <name> will be modified to point to the machine code, and <name>'s first parameter will point to the generic execution procedure.

DP (d-p)   <f>

Stack: > > > **addr**

User variable containing a pointer to the next free memory location at the top of the dictionary. The pointer value may be left on the stack by **HERE** and incremented by **ALLOT**. At execution, the location of the pointer within the user area will be left on the stack.

Reference: 4.2, 6.3, 6.4, 6.9

DPL (d-p-l)   <f>

Stack: > > > **addr**

User variable containing the number of digits to the right of a "period" character in double-precision input. Numbers input without a period will leave the variable with a default value of −1. At execution, the location of the value within the user area will be left on the stack.

Reference: 9.5

DR0 (d-r-zero)   <f>

Installation-dependent routine to preset **OFFSET** to zero to select drive 0 as the current disk.

Reference: 10.1

DR1 (d-r-one)   <f>

Installation-dependent routine to preset **OFFSET** to select drive 1 as the current disk.

Reference: 10.1

DRIVE   <z>

Stack: > > > **addr**

System variable containing the number of the disk drive most recently used. The maximum drive number is specified within the boot-up literal area. At execution, the location of the value will be left on the stack.

Reference: 10.1, B.1

DROP   <f,s>

Stack: n > > >

Remove the top single-precision value from the stack.

Reference: 1.4

DU< (d-u-less-than)   <x>

Stack: ud1 ud2 > > > f

Leave a true flag if the unsigned double-precision number **ud1** is less than **ud2**. Otherwise, leave a false flag.

DUMP   <f>

Stack: addr n > > >

Output the contents of **n** bytes of memory, beginning at location **addr**. Both addresses and byte contents will be output using the current I/O numeric base.

Note that **DUMP** is listed in the standard fig-FORTH glossary, but is not shown in the model.

DUP   <f,s>

Stack: n > > > n n

Leave two copies of the top stack value **n**.

Reference: 1.2, 1.4

ELSE   <f,s>

Stack: **addr1 n1 > > > addr2 n2**   (compilation)

Format: **: <name> ... IF ... ELSE ... ENDIF ... ;**   <f>
        : <name> ... IF ... ELSE ... THEN ... ;   <f,s>

Immediate word to compile the intermediate portion of a conditional.

During compilation of <name>'s dictionary definition, **ELSE** executes immediately due to its precedence bit. A pointer to the run-time unconditional branching routine is compiled into <name>'s parameter field, along with a dummy offset at **addr2**. The dummy offset previously compiled at **addr1** by **IF** is replaced with the actual offset from the start of the conditional to the first parameter beyond **addr2**. The operand **n1** and result **n2** are error check values.

During later execution of <name>, the conditional branching run-time routine associated with **IF** will test and remove the top stack value as a flag. If true, the components of the true branch will be executed and the second offset used to ignore the remainder of the conditional. If the flag is false, the first offset will be used to transfer execution to the start of the false branch.

Reference: 5.2

Colon Definition:
: ELSE

2 ?PAIRS	Test the error check value **n1**. If not equal to 2, issue an error message.
COMPILE BRANCH	Compile a pointer to the run-time routine in the next available dictionary location.
HERE	Leave the current dictionary pointer **addr2**.
0 ,	Compile a dummy offset in the next available dictionary location.
SWAP	Exchange **addr1** and **addr2**.
2	Leave an error check value.
[COMPILE] ENDIF	Use ENDIF to test the check value, and to recompile the dummy offset at **addr1**.

2	Leave an error check value **n2**.
; IMMEDIATE	Terminate definition, set precedence.

◇   ◇   ◇

EMIT   <f,s>

Stack: c > > >

Installation-dependent routine to send the ASCII character **c** to the terminal. The fig-FORTH user variable **OUT** is incremented for each character.

Reference: 3.3, 9.1, 9.3

◇   ◇   ◇

EMPTY-BUFFERS   <f,s>

Mark all mass storage buffers in memory as empty, without saving the contents on disk.

Reference: 10.2

Colon Definition:
: EMPTY-BUFFERS

FIRST LIMIT	Leave the endpoint addresses of the buffer area.
OVER –	Duplicate the lower address, and calculate the number of bytes.
ERASE	Place "null" (ASCII 00) characters in all bytes.
;	Terminate definition.

ENCLOSE   <f>

Stack: **addr1 c** > > > **addr1 n1 n2 n3**

Used by **WORD** to scan text beginning at location **addr1** and delimited by the ASCII character code **c**. An ASCII "null" will be treated as an unconditional delimiter.

The starting address **addr1** is left as a result, along with the byte offset **n1** to the first non-delimiter, **n2** to the first delimiter after a valid character, and **n3** to the first character not scanned.

◇   ◇   ◇

END   < f >

Stack: **f** > > >   (run-time)
   addr n > > >   (compilation)

Format: **:** < name > ... **BEGIN** ... **END** ... **;**

Immediate word to complete compilation of an indefinite loop which contains a post-pass test for execution completion. Equivalent to **UNTIL**.

During compilation of < name >'s dictionary definition, **END** executes immediately due to its precedence bit. A pointer to the run-time conditional branching routine is compiled into < name >'s parameter field. The location **addr** left by **BEGIN** is used to calculate and compile an offset back to the top of the loop. The operand **n** is used as an error check value.

During later execution of < name >, the conditional branching run-time routine associated with **END** will test and remove the top stack value **f**. If true, execution continues with the next component word following the loop. If the flag is false, the offset will be used to transfer execution to the top of the loop.

Reference: 5.4, 12.4

Colon Definition:
: END
   [COMPILE] UNTIL   Use the equivalent definition.
; IMMEDIATE   Terminate definition, set precedence.

◇   ◇   ◇

END-CODE   < x >

Format: **CODE** < name > **mn END-CODE**

Terminate compilation of an assembly mnemonic definition for < name >. The context vocabulary is reset from **ASSEMBLER** to the current vocabulary.

Reference: 8.2

ENDIF   \<f\>

Stack: **addr n** \> \> \>   (compilation)

Format: **:** \<**name**\> ... **IF** ... **ENDIF** ... **;**
         : \<**name**\> ... **IF** ... **ELSE** ... **ENDIF** ... **;**

Immediate word to complete compilation of a conditional. Equivalent to **THEN**.

During compilation of \<**name**\>'s dictionary definition, **ENDIF** executes immediately due to its precedence bit. The dummy offset previously compiled by **IF** or **ELSE** at **addr** is replaced with the actual offset from **addr** to the current dictionary location. The operand **n** is an error check value.

During later execution of \<**name**\>, the conditional branching routine associated with **IF** will test and remove the top stack value as a flag. If true, the components of the true branch will be executed; the remainder of the conditional, if any, will be ignored. If the flag is false, the initial offset will be used to transfer execution to the false branch; if no false branch exists, the true branch will simply be ignored.

Reference: 5.2, 12.4

Colon Definition:
: ENDIF

?COMP	Issue an error message if not compiling.
2 ?PAIRS	Test the error check value **n**. If not equal to 2, issue an error message.
HERE	Leave the current dictionary pointer.
OVER	Copy **addr**.
–	Calculate the offset.
SWAP !	Compile the offset at **addr**.
; IMMEDIATE	Terminate definition, set precedence.

ERASE   \<f\>

Stack: **addr n** \> \> \>

Place "null" (ASCII 00) characters in **n** consecutive bytes in memory, beginning at **addr**. In some versions of fig-FORTH, bytes will be filled only if **n** is greater than zero.

Reference: 3.1

Colon Definition:
: ERASE
   0 FILL   Fill **n** bytes with zeros.
;   Terminate definition.

  ◇   ◇   ◇

ERROR   \<f\>

Stack: **n1** > > > **n2 n3**   (fig-FORTH model)
      n1 > > > **n3 n2**   (8080/Z-80 disk input)
      n1 > > >   (8080/Z-80 terminal input)

Perform the error notification and recovery routine for error number **n1**, in accordance with the value stored in user variable **WARNING**.

If the value of **WARNING** is −1, the installation-dependent **(ABORT)** routine will be executed.

If **WARNING** has a value of 1, error message **n1** will be output from the disk. Fig-FORTH presumes that source code screens 4 and 5 on drive 0 contain the error messages, on individual lines specified as an offset **n1** from line 0 of screen 4. If **WARNING** has a value of zero, only the error number **n1** will be output. In either case, the stacks will be cleared and control returned to the terminal for further input.

The fig-FORTH model indicates that the value **n2** of user variable **IN** and the value **n3** of **BLK** will be placed on the stack. The 8080/Z-80 version reverses the order of the two values, which are left only if the input stream was being taken from the disk.

Reference: 12.4

Colon Definition:
: ERROR   NOTE: Model definition
   WARNING @   Fetch the value of the user variable.
   0<   Leave a true flag if the value is −1.
   IF (ABORT) ENDIF   True — execute installation-
                         dependent error routine.

HERE	Leave a pointer to the word buffer containing the input word.
COUNT TYPE	Output the word from the buffer.
." ?"	Output a question mark.
MESSAGE	Output the error number **n1**, and if **WARNING** is non-zero output the line **n1** lines from the start of screen 4 on drive 0.
SP!	Reinitialize the parameter stack pointer.
IN @ BLK @	Fetch the input byte offset and current block number.
QUIT	Restart the interpreter loop.
;	Terminate definition.

◇   ◇   ◇

EXECUTE   <f,s>

Stack: **addr** > > >

Execute the word whose code field address **addr** is on the stack.

Reference: 12.1, 12.2

◇   ◇   ◇

EXIT   <s>

Format: **:** < name > ... **EXIT** ... **;**

Terminate execution of < name > . **EXIT** must not appear within an indexed loop.

◇   ◇   ◇

EXPECT   <f,s>

Stack: **addr n** > > >

Transfer a text string from the terminal to memory, beginning at location **addr**. Transfer continues until **n** characters have been input, or a "return" keypress is detected. One or more "null" characters

(ASCII 00) are appended to the end of the text string.

For FORTH-79, no characters will be transmitted if **n** is not greater than zero.

Reference: 9.4

Colon Definition:
: EXPECT

OVER +	Calculate the location of the next byte past a string space of **n** characters.
OVER	Leave a copy of **addr** as an initial index.
DO	Begin an indexed loop.
KEY DUP	Get and copy an input character c.
14 +ORIGIN @	Fetch the terminal's backspace character code from the boot-up literal area.
=	Compare to the input.
IF	Outer true branch — c is a backspace.
DROP	Drop c from the stack.
8 OVER	Leave a backspace code and copy **addr**.
I =	True if c was the first character.
DUP	Copy the flag.
R >	Move the loop index from the return stack to the parameter stack.
2 − +	Adjust the index, decrementing by 2 if c was the first character, and by 1 otherwise.
>R	Move the loop index back to the return stack.
−	Subtract the flag from **addr**.
ELSE	Outer false branch — c not a backspace.
DUP	Copy the character.
13 =	True if c is a "return".
IF	Inner true branch — c is a "return".
LEAVE	Exit the loop at the end of the pass.
DROP	Drop the "return" from the stack.
BL	Leave a "blank" code for printing.
0	Leave a "null" code for storage.

ELSE	Inner false branch — neither a backspace nor a "return".
DUP	Copy c for printing.
ENDIF	Terminate inner conditional.
I C!	Store the non-backspace character or "null".
0 I 1+ !	Store a "null" after the present end of the text.
ENDIF	Terminate outer conditional.
EMIT	Output the character to the terminal.
LOOP	Terminate indexed loop.
DROP	Drop **addr** from the stack.
;	Terminate definition.

◇   ◇   ◇

FENCE   \<f\>

Stack: > > > **addr**

User variable containing a pointer to the lowest unprotected memory location. Any attempt to **FORGET** words below the location indicated by **FENCE** will cause an error. At execution, the location of the pointer within the user area will be left on the stack.

Reference: 6.3, 6.9, B.1

◇   ◇   ◇

FILL   \<f,s\>

Stack: **addr n b** > > >

Place the value **b** in **n** consecutive memory bytes, beginning at location **addr**.

For FORTH-79 and some versions of fig-FORTH, **FILL** will not store any characters if **n** is not greater than zero.

Reference: 3.1

Colon Definition:
: FILL

SWAP >R	Move **n** to the return stack.
OVER	Copy **addr**.

C!	Save **b** at **addr**.
DUP 1+	Copy **addr** and increment one copy.
R> 1 –	Move **n** back to the parameter stack and decrement it.
CMOVE	Move **n–1** bytes, beginning with **addr**, to the area of memory beginning at **addr+1**.
;	Terminate definition.

FIND   <s>

Stack: > > > **addr**

Leave the code field address of the next blank-delimited word < **name** > from the input stream. If no match is found in the context vocabulary, a code field of 0000 is left.
See –**FIND**.

Reference: 7.5

FIRST   <f>

Stack: > > > **n**

System constant to leave the header address of the lowest mass storage buffer in memory.

Reference: 6.10

FLD   <f>

Stack: > > > **addr**

User variable containing a value for output field formatting. Presently unused in fig-FORTH. At execution, the location of the value within the user area will be left on the stack.

FLUSH   <z>

Write to the disk the contents of all mass storage buffers which
have their update bits set to 1.
   See **SAVE-BUFFERS**.

Reference: 10.3, 11.3

FORGET   <f,s>

Format: **FORGET** < name >

   Delete < **name** > and all later additions to the dictionary, regardless of their vocabulary. Send an error message if < **name** > is within
the protected portion of the dictionary. Fig-FORTH requires that
the context and current vocabularies be identical, and contain
< **name** >; FORTH-79 requires < **name** > to be in the current
vocabulary.
   FORGET can only be used for execution, and must not be used as
a component word in colon definitions.

Reference: 4.3.2, 6.3, 7.4, 11.4.2, 12.4, B.1

Colon Definition:
: FORGET
   CURRENT @
   CONTEXT @   Fetch the vocabulary pointers.
   − 24 ?ERROR   Compare by subtraction. If not
                                 identical, issue an error message.
   [COMPILE] '   Leave the parameter field address of
                                 the next word < **name** > from the
                                 input stream.
   DUP   Copy the address.
   FENCE @   Fetch the pointer to the lowest
                                 unprotected dictionary location.
   < 21 ?ERROR   If < **name** > is within the protected
                                 area, issue an error message.
   DUP   Copy the parameter field address
                                 again.

NFA DP !	Set the dictionary pointer to the start of < name > 's definition.
LFA @	Fetch the link field contents of < name >.
CURRENT @	Fetch the address within the vocabulary defining word containing the pointer to the most recent name field.
!	Store the pointer to the name field immediately preceding < name > in the current vocabulary.
;	Terminate definition.

◇   ◇   ◇

FORTH   <f,s>

Immediate vocabulary defining word to select the **FORTH** vocabulary as the context vocabulary for dictionary searches.

All user-defined vocabularies are ultimately linked to **FORTH**. Any search of a user-defined vocabulary will also cause **FORTH** to be searched.

Reference: 7.1, 7.4, 7.5, 8.2, 11.2, 12.4, B.1, B.2

◇   ◇   ◇

HERE   <f,s>

Stack: > > > addr

Leave a pointer to the next available dictionary location.

Reference: 4.2, 6.3

Colon Definition:
: HERE

DP @	Fetch the dictionary pointer from user variable DP.
;	Terminate definition.

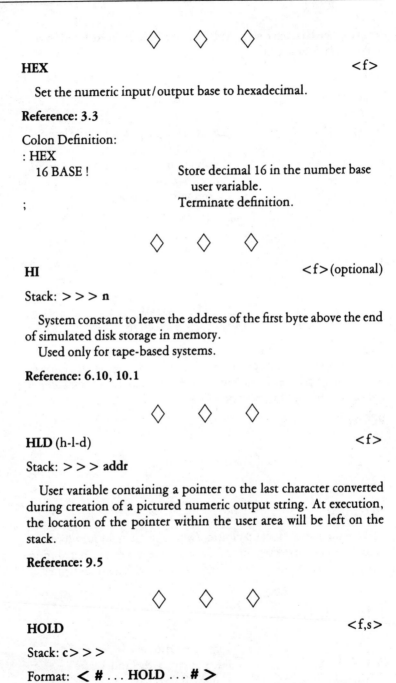

HEX   <f>

　　Set the numeric input/output base to hexadecimal.

Reference: 3.3

Colon Definition:
: HEX
　　16 BASE !   Store decimal 16 in the number base
　　　　　　　　　　　　　　　　　　 user variable.
　　;   Terminate definition.

HI   <f>(optional)

Stack: > > > n

　　System constant to leave the address of the first byte above the end
of simulated disk storage in memory.
　　Used only for tape-based systems.

Reference: 6.10, 10.1

HLD (h-l-d)   <f>

Stack: > > > addr

　　User variable containing a pointer to the last character converted
during creation of a pictured numeric output string. At execution,
the location of the pointer within the user area will be left on the
stack.

Reference: 9.5

HOLD   <f,s>

Stack: c> > >

Format: **< # ... HOLD ... # >**

Insert the character with ASCII code c into the next location of a pictured output text string.

Reference: 9.5

Colon Definition:
: HOLD

−1 HLD +!	Decrement the pointer to the latest character.
HLD @	Fetch the pointer to the new location.
C!	Store character c.
;	Terminate definition.

$$\diamondsuit \quad \diamondsuit \quad \diamondsuit$$

I   <f,s>

Stack: > > > n

Formats: : < name > ... **DO** ... **I** ... **LOOP** ... ;
       : < name > ... **DO** ... **I** ... **+LOOP** ... ;

Leave the current index of the innermost loop in which **I** appears.
All FORTH-79 loop parameters use signed single-precision values. If the loop index is used to represent a memory address, proper account of the sign bit must be made.

Reference: 5.3

$$\diamondsuit \quad \diamondsuit \quad \diamondsuit$$

ID. (i-d-dot)   <f>

Stack: addr > > >

Print the name of the definition whose name field is at location **addr**. If some characters of the word name were omitted during compilation, indicate each omitted character with an underscore.

Reference: 7.2, 8.1, 9.3

Colon Definition:
: ID.

PAD	Leave a pointer to the text buffer.
32 95 FILL	Fill 32 bytes with "underscore" (ASCII 95) characters.

DUP PFA LFA	Copy **addr** and leave the link field address.
OVER	Copy **addr**.
–	Calculate the length of the name field, as stored.
PAD SWAP	Leave the length above a pointer to the text buffer.
CMOVE	Move the name field contents to the text buffer.
31 AND	Mask the upper 3 bits of the length byte contents, using the constant (01FH).
TYPE SPACE	Output the string.
;	Terminate definition.

◇   ◇   ◇

IF   <f,s>

Stack: **f> > >**   (run-time)
     > > > addr n   (compilation)

Formats: **: <name>** ... **IF** ... **ENDIF** ... **;**   <f>
        : <name> ... **IF** ... **ELSE** ... **ENDIF** ...**;**   <f>
        : <name> ... **IF** ... **THEN** ... **;**
        : <name> ... **IF** ... **ELSE** ... **THEN** ... **;**

Immediate word to begin compilation of a conditional.

During compilation of <name>'s dictionary definition, IF executes immediately due to its precedence bit. A pointer to the run-time conditional branching routine is compiled into <name>'s parameter field along with a dummy offset at **addr**. The offset will be recompiled when the first ELSE, ENDIF, or THEN component is encountered later in the compilation process for <name>. The result **n** is an error check value.

During later execution of <name>, the conditional branching run-time routine will test and remove the top stack value **f** as a flag. The run-time routines and offsets compiled by the immediate conditional words will be used to direct execution between two possible paths. For **IF-ELSE-ENDIF** or **IF-ELSE-THEN** sequences, only the component words between IF and ELSE will be executed if the flag is true; if false, only the components following ELSE will be executed. For **IF-ENDIF** or **IF-THEN** sequences, the component words within the conditional will be executed only if the flag is true.

FORTH-79 uses **THEN** to terminate conditionals. Fig-FORTH may use either **THEN** or **ENDIF** with equivalent results.

Reference: 5.2, 5.5, 12.4

Colon Definition:
: IF
    COMPILE 0BRANCH   Compile a pointer to the run-time routine in the next available dictionary location.

    HERE   Leave the current dictionary pointer as **addr**.

    0 ,   Compile a dummy offset in the next available dictionary location.

    2   Leave an error check value **n**.
; IMMEDIATE   Terminate definition, set precedence.

IMMEDIATE   <f,s>

Set the precedence bit of the most recent definition. Words which have been marked as immediate will execute during compilation. An immediate word may be compiled as a component in a definition only if preceded by **[COMPILE]**.

Reference: 5.5, 8.1

Colon Definition:
: IMMEDIATE
    LATEST   Leave a pointer to the name field of the most recent addition in the current vocabulary.

    64 TOGGLE   Toggle the length byte, using the constant (40H).
;   Terminate definition.

IN   <f>

Stack: > > > **addr**

User variable containing an offset pointer corresponding to the next character in the input stream. At execution, the location of the pointer within the user area will be left on the stack.
  See **> IN**.

Reference: 9.4, 12.2

INDEX   <f>

Stack: **n1 n2 > > >**

Output the first lines of screens **n1** through **n2** to the terminal. Terminate the output if the "break" key is detected.

Reference: 11.2

Colon Definition:
: INDEX

12 EMIT CR	Output a "form feed" (ASCII code 12), followed by a carriage return and line feed.
1+ SWAP	Increment **n2**, and exchange loop parameter positions.
DO	Begin an indexed loop.
CR	Output a carriage return and line feed.
I 3 .R SPACE	Output the screen number and a space.
0 I .LINE	Output the first line of a screen.
?TERMINAL	Leave a true flag if "break" is detected; otherwise, leave a false flag.
IF LEAVE ENDIF	If "break" detected, exit the loop at the end of the pass.
LOOP	Increment index, check for completion.
;	Terminate definition.

INTERPRET   <f>

Invoke the fig-FORTH text interpreter to parse and execute or compile individual words from the input stream. The input stream may either be a line of text from the terminal or the contents of a mass storage buffer holding source code from the disk.

Each blank-delimited word in the input stream is compared to word names in the current and context vocabularies. If a match is found, its length byte's contents and the value of **STATE** are used to determine whether to execute or compile the input word. If no match is found, the word is converted to numeric input in accordance with the current input/output numeric base, saving the position of any embedded "period" character.

Interpretation continues word-by-word until the end of the input stream (designated by one or more "null" characters) is detected. If no error has occurred, further input will be accepted. If the stack is out of bounds or if an input word neither matches a defined word name nor can be converted to a valid numeric value, interpretation is aborted.

Reference: 12.2

Colon Definition:
: INTERPRET
  BEGIN   Begin an indefinite loop.
    –FIND   Copy the next blank-delimited word
                                 from the input stream to the word
                                 buffer and search the current and
                                 context vocabularies for a match. If
                                 found, leave the word's parameter
                                 field address, the contents of its
                                 name field length byte, and a true
                                 flag; otherwise leave only a false
                                 flag.
    IF   Outer true branch — match found.
      STATE @   Fetch the user variable's value.
      <   Leave a true flag if in the compilation
                                 state and the word's precedence bit
                                 is set to zero.
      IF   Inner true branch — compiling.

CFA ,	Compile a pointer to the matching word's code field into the next cell at the top of the dictionary.
ELSE	Inner false branch — execution state or immediate word.
CFA EXECUTE	Execute the matching word.
ENDIF	Terminate inner conditional.
?STACK	Issue an error message if the stack is out of bounds.
ELSE	Outer false branch — no match found.
HERE	Leave a pointer to the input word in the buffer.
NUMBER	If possible, convert the word to a double-precision numeric value in the current input/output base and leave it on the stack. Otherwise, issue an error message.
DPL @ 1+	Increment the decimal pointer for use as a flag. The resulting value will be zero only if no "period" character was located.
IF	Inner true branch — "period" found.
[COMPILE] DLITERAL	If in the compilation state, compile the double-precision number on the stack into the top of the dictionary, along with run-time pointers. If executing, no effect.
ELSE	Inner false branch — no "period" found.
DROP	Drop the high-order half of the converted double-precision number.
[COMPILE] LITERAL	If in the compilation state, compile the single-precision number on the stack into the top of the dictionary, along with a run-time pointer. If executing, no effect.
ENDIF	Terminate inner conditional.

?STACK	Issue an error message if the stack is out of bounds.
ENDIF	Terminate outer conditional.
AGAIN	Repeat the loop until an error condition or execution of "null" forces termination.
;	Terminate definition.

J   <s>

Stack: > > > n

Format: : <name> ... DO ... DO ... J ... LOOP ... LOOP
 ... ;

Copy the current loop index n of the next outer loop in which J appears.

Reference: 5.3

KEY   <f,s>

Stack: > > > c

Installation-dependent routine to input a character with ASCII code c from the terminal.

Reference: 3.3, 9.1, 9.4

LATEST   <f>

Stack: > > > addr

Leave the name field of the most recent addition to the current vocabulary.

Reference: 7.3, 8.1

Colon Definition:
: LATEST

CURRENT @	Fetch a pointer to a location within a vocabulary defining word's definition.
@	Fetch that defining word's pointer to the name field of its most recent addition.
;	Terminate definition.

◇   ◇   ◇

LEAVE   \<f,s\>

Formats: : \<name\> ... DO ... LEAVE ... LOOP ... ;
          : \<name\> ... DO ... LEAVE ... +LOOP ... ;

Set the limit value of an indexed loop to the current index value. The loop will precede normally until the next encounter with **LOOP** or **+LOOP**, when it will terminate.

Reference: 5.3

◇   ◇   ◇

LFA (l-f-a)   \<f\>

Stack: **addr1 > > > addr2**

Leave the link field address **addr2** of the definition whose parameter field starts at **addr1**.

Reference: 7.2

Colon Definition:
: LFA

4 –	Subtract 4 bytes from the parameter field address.
;	Terminate definition.

◇   ◇   ◇

LIMIT   \<f\>

Stack: **> > > n**

System constant to leave the address of the first byte above the mass storage buffer area in memory.

In systems without disk storage, memory beginning at **LIMIT** may be used to simulate disk blocks.

Reference: 6.10, 10.2.1

LIST   <f,s>

Stack: **n** > > >

Output the ASCII text of source code screen **n**, and update the screen number user variable **SCR**. The numeric I/O base is set to decimal.

In some versions of fig-FORTH, the output can be ended prematurely by the terminal's "break" key.

Reference: 11.2

Colon Definition:
: LIST

DECIMAL	Set the I/O base for decimal.
CR	Output a carriage return and line feed.
DUP SCR !	Store a copy of **n** in the user variable.
." SCR # " .	Output a message and **n**.
16 0	Leave line number loop parameters.
DO	Begin an indexed loop.
CR	Send a carriage return and line feed.
I 3 .R SPACE	Output the line number and a space.
I SCR @	Leave the line and screen number.
.LINE	Send the line, without trailing blanks.
LOOP	Terminate indexed loop.
CR	Send a carriage return and line feed.
;	Terminate definition.

LIT   <f>

Stack: > > > **n**

Compiled by **LITERAL** or **DLITERAL** within a colon definition as the run-time procedure to move an in-line literal value **n** to the stack.

Reference: 5.5

◇   ◇   ◇

LITERAL   <f,s>

Stack: **n > > >**   (compilation)

Immediate word used by the text interpreter and "tick" to compile a single-precision value as an in-line literal.

During compilation of a colon definition, the top stack value **n** is compiled as a literal preceded by a pointer to the associated run-time routine. During later execution of the definition, the literal value will be placed on the stack.

LITERAL has no effect when encountered during execution.

Reference: 5.5, 7.2, 7.3

Colon Definition:
: LITERAL

STATE @	Fetch the compilation state user variable.
IF	True branch — compilation state.
COMPILE LIT	Compile a pointer to the run-time routine into the next available dictionary location.
,	Compile **n** into the next available dictionary location.
ENDIF	Terminate conditional.
; IMMEDIATE	Terminate definition, set precedence.

◇   ◇   ◇

LO   <f>(optional)

Stack: **> > > n**

System constant to leave the address of the first byte of simulated disk storage in memory.

Reference: 6.10, 10.1

LOAD   <f,s>

Stack: **n** > > >

Assign source code screen **n** as the input stream, and interpret its contents.

In a source code screen being interpreted, **LOAD** will cause interpretation of that screen to be suspended until the newly referenced screen **n** has been interpreted.

Reference: 11.4, 12.2

Colon Definition:
: LOAD
>   BLK @ >R   Save the current block number on the
>   return stack.
>   IN @ >R   Save the current input offset pointer.
>   0 IN !   Reset the input offset pointer.
>   B/SCR * BLK !   Calculate and save the number of the
>   first block of screen **n**.
>   INTERPRET   Parse and execute or compile the
>   input stream until exhausted.
>   R> IN ! R> BLK !   Restore the previous offset pointer
>   and block number.
> ;   Terminate definition.

LOOP   <f,s>

Stack: **addr n** > > >   (compilation)

Format: **:** < name > ... **DO** ... **LOOP** ... **;**

Immediate word to complete compilation of an indexed loop using an implicit index increment of 1.

During compilation of < name >'s colon definition, **LOOP** executes immediately due to its precedence bit. In turn, a pointer to the run-time routine associated with **LOOP** is compiled into < name >'s parameter field. The **addr** operand, left by **DO**, is used to calculate and compile an offset back to the first word of the loop. The **n** operand, also left by **DO**, is used for compilation error-checking.

During later execution of < **name** > , the run-time routine associated with **LOOP** executes by incrementing the loop index by one. If the incremented index is less than the limit parameter, the in-line offset is used to transfer execution back to the top of the loop. If the incremented index equals or exceeds the limit value, the offset is ignored; execution continues outside the loop after dropping the loop parameters from the return stack.

Reference: 5.3, 5.5, 12.4

Colon Definition:
: LOOP

3 ?PAIRS	Test the error check value **n**. If not equal to 3, issue an error message.
COMPILE (LOOP)	Compile a pointer to the run-time routine into the next location in < **name** >'s parameter field.
BACK	Use **addr** to calculate the backwards offset to the top of the loop, and compile it into < **name** >'s definition.
; IMMEDIATE	Terminate definition, set precedence.

$$\Diamond \qquad \Diamond \qquad \Diamond$$

M* (m-times)   <f>

Stack: **n1 n2 > > > d**

Leave the signed double-precision number product of **n1** and **n2**.

Reference: 2.4

Colon Definition:
: M*

OVER OVER	Copy **n1** and **n2**.
XOR >R	Move sign value to return stack.
ABS SWAP ABS	Leave unsigned equivalents of operands.
U*	Calculate the unsigned double-precision number product.
R> D+−	Move sign value back from return stack, set sign of product.
;	Terminate definition.

M/ (m-divide)   \<f\>

Stack: **d n1** > > > **n2 n3**

Leave the remainder **n2** and signed quotient **n3** of the double-precision number d divided by **n1**. The remainder will have the same sign as **d**.

Reference: 2.4

Colon Definition:
: M/
OVER >R	Move a copy of the high-order half of d to the return stack.
>R	Save **n1** on the return stack.
DABS	Leave the absolute value of d.
R ABS	Copy **n1**, leave the absolute value.
U/	Leave the unsigned remainder and quotient.
R>	Move **n1** back from the return stack.
R	Copy the high-order half of d.
XOR +−	Find the sign of the quotient.
SWAP	Exchange positions of remainder and quotient.
R> +−	Use the high-order half of d to set the sign of the remainder.
SWAP	Exchange positions of remainder and quotient again.
;	Terminate definition.

M/MOD (m-divide-mod)   \<f\>

Stack: **ud1 u1** > > > **u2 ud2**

Using unsigned values, leave the remainder **u2** and double-precision quotient **ud2** of the division of double-precision number **ud1** by **u1**.
Reference: 2.4

Colon Definition:
: M/MOD

>R	Move divisor **u1** to the return stack.
0 R U/	Calculate the high-order portion using the high-order half of **ud1** and **u1**, leaving a remainder and the high-order half of **ud2**.
R>	Move **u1** from the return stack.
SWAP >R	Move the high-order half of **ud2** to the return stack.
U/	Calculate the low-order portion, leaving the remainder **u2** and the low-order half of **ud2**.
R>	Move the high-order half of **ud2** back to the stack.
;	Terminate definition.

◇   ◇   ◇

MAX   <f,s>

Stack: **n1 n2 > > > n3**

Leave the maximum **n3** of signed numbers **n1** and **n2**.

Reference: 2.2

Colon Definition:
: MAX

OVER OVER	Duplicate **n1** and **n2**.
<	True if **n1** is less than **n2**.
IF SWAP ENDIF	If true, exchange positions so that lesser value is on top.
DROP	Drop lesser value.
;	Terminate definition.

◇   ◇   ◇

MESSAGE   <f>

Stack: **n > > >**

Output the error number **n**. If the value of user variable **WARNING** is non-zero, output an associated message from disk. Fig-FORTH presumes that source code screens 4 and 5 on drive 0 contain system error messages, on individual lines specified as an offset **n** from line 0 of screen 4.

Colon Definition:
: MESSAGE

WARNING @	Fetch the value of the user variable. A value of 1 indicates that a disk is present.
IF	Outer true branch — disk available.
−DUP	Duplicate **n**.
IF	Inner true branch — non-zero **n**.
4	Leave screen number for the start of error messages.
OFFSET @	Fetch the number of the first block on the current disk.
B / SCR / −	Leave screen number relative to start of current disk.
.LINE	Output line **n** of the screen.
ENDIF	Terminate inner conditional.
ELSE	Outer false branch — no disk.
." MSG # " .	Output the caption and error number.
ENDIF	Terminate outer conditional.
;	Terminate definition.

◇   ◇   ◇

MIN   <f,s>

Stack: **n1 n2 > > > n3**

Leave the minimum **n3** of signed numbers **n1** and **n2**.

Reference: 2.2

Colon Definition:
: MIN

OVER OVER	Copy **n1** and **n2**.
>	True if **n1** is greater than **n2**.
IF SWAP ENDIF	If true, exchange positions so that greater value is on top.
DROP	Drop the greater value.
;	Terminate definition.

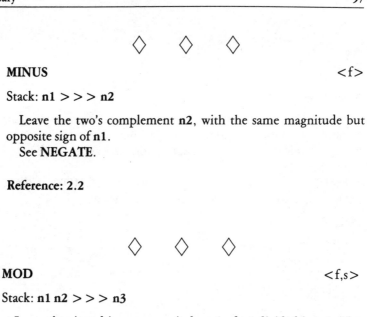

MINUS   \<f\>

Stack: **n1** > > > **n2**

Leave the two's complement **n2**, with the same magnitude but opposite sign of **n1**.
See **NEGATE**.

Reference: 2.2

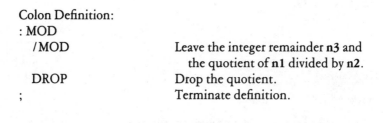

MOD   \<f,s\>

Stack: **n1 n2** > > > **n3**

Leave the signed integer remainder **n3** of **n1** divided by **n2**. The remainder has the same sign as **n1**.

Reference: 2.2

Colon Definition:
: MOD
   /MOD   Leave the integer remainder **n3** and
                                 the quotient of **n1** divided by **n2**.

   DROP   Drop the quotient.
;   Terminate definition.

MON   \<f\>

Installation-dependent routine to exit to the system monitor. If possible, the necessary values for a later re-entry to FORTH will be saved.

Reference: 12.2

MOVE   <f,s>

Stack: **addr1 addr2 n** > > >

   Move **n** 16-bit cells, beginning at **addr1**, to the memory locations
beginning at **addr2**. The move proceeds from low to high memory.
For 16-bit cell-addressing processors, **addr1** and **addr2** must be on
cell boundaries.
   For FORTH-79 and some versions of fig-FORTH, **MOVE** will not
move any cell contents if **n** is not greater than zero.

Reference: 3.1

NEGATE   <s>

Stack: **n1** > > > **n2**

   Leave the two's complement **n2**, with the same magnitude but
opposite sign of **n1**.
   See **MINUS**.

Reference: 2.2

NFA (n-f-a)   <f>

Stack: **addr1** > > > **addr2**

   Leave the name field address **addr2** of the definition whose parameter field starts at **addr1**.

Reference: 7.2

Colon Definition:
: NFA
    5 –   Calculate the location of the last
                      name field character.

    –1 TRAVERSE   Leave the address of the first name
                      field byte.

;   Terminate definition.

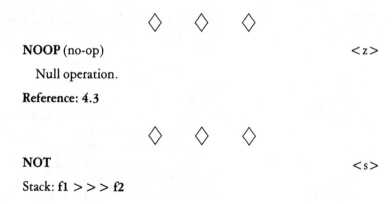

NOOP (no-op)   <z>

Null operation.

Reference: 4.3

NOT   <s>

Stack: **f1 > > > f2**

Reverse flag **f1** to **f2**. For a numeric operand, equivalent to **0=** .

Reference: 5.1

NUMBER   <f>

Stack: **addr > > > d**

Convert a dimensioned text string with a count byte at location **addr** to its signed numeric equivalent, using the current numeric I/O base. If a "period" character (denoting a double-precision value) is encountered within the string, leave its relative position in user variable **DPL**.

If the input is not convertible to a valid numeric value, an error message will be output.

Reference: 9.5, 12.2, B.1

Colon Definition:
: NUMBER

0 0	Initialize two stack positions to serve as a double-precision accumulator.
ROT DUP	Leave two copies of **addr** on top.
1+ C@	Fetch the first text character.
45 =	True if character is a minus sign.
DUP >R	Move a copy of the flag to the return stack.

+	Add the flag to the text address, to point to the first non-sign character.
−1	Leave an initial value for **DPL**.
BEGIN	Begin an indefinite loop.
DPL !	Save the decimal location.
(NUMBER)	Convert all possible characters to digit equivalents, and leave the accumulated double-precision number and a pointer to the first unconvertible character.
DUP C@	Duplicate the pointer and fetch the unconvertible character.
BL −	Leave a true flag if character is not a "blank".
WHILE	If not a blank, continue.
DUP C@	Duplicate the pointer and fetch the unconvertible character again.
46 −	Leave a true flag if character not a "period".
0 ?ERROR	Issue an error message if the character is not a "period".
0	If a period, initialize **DPL**.
REPEAT	Repeat the loop for remaining digits.
DROP	Drop the remaining address from the stack.
R>	Move the sign flag from the return stack.
IF DMINUS ENDIF	Negate the value if a minus sign was detected as the first character.
;	Terminate definition.

◇   ◇   ◇

OFFSET   <f>

Stack: > > > **addr**

User variable containing the block number of the lowest block on the currently-enabled disk drive. The value is used by **BUFFER** to calculate the absolute equivalent of a block number specified relative to the start of the current disk. At execution, the location of the value within the user area will be left on the stack.

Reference: 10.1, B.1

OR   <f,s>

Stack: **n1 n2 > > > n3**

Leave the bit-by-bit logical "or" **n3** of **n1** and **n2**. The i-th bit of **n3** will be set to 1 if the i-th bits of either or both **n1** or **n2** are 1.

Reference: 2.5

OUT   <f>

Stack: **> > > addr**

User variable containing an offset pointer corresponding to the last output character. The pointer is incremented by **EMIT** and may be used or changed for output formatting. At execution, the location of the pointer within the user area will be left on the stack.

Reference: 9.3

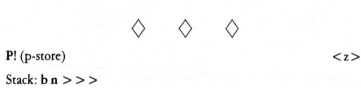

OVER   <f,s>

Stack: **n1 n2 > > > n1 n2 n1**

Leave a copy of the second stack value **n1** on top of the stack.

Reference: 1.4

P! (p-store)   <z>

Stack: **b n > > >**

Output byte **b** to port **n**.

Reference: 3.3, 9.1.1

◇   ◇   ◇

P@ (p-fetch)   <z>

Stack: **n > > > b**

Input byte **b** from port **n**.

Reference: 3.3, 9.1.1

◇   ◇   ◇

PAD   <f,s>

Stack: **> > > addr**

Leave a pointer to the start of the text buffer, which "floats" a fixed distance above the top of the dictionary.

Reference: 6.5, 9.3

Colon Definition:
: PAD
   HERE   Leave a pointer to the current top of
                    the dictionary.
   68 +   Increment the pointer to the text
                    buffer.
   ;   Terminate definition.

◇   ◇   ◇

PFA (p-f-a)   <f>

Stack: **addr1 > > > addr2**

Leave the parameter field address **addr2** of the definition whose name field starts at **addr1**.

Reference: 7.2

Colon Definition:
: PFA
   1 TRAVERSE   Leave the address of the last name
                    field byte.
   5 +   Increment the pointer to the first byte
                    of the parameter field.
   ;   Terminate definition.

PICK   <s>

Stack: **n1 > > > n2**

Leave the contents **n2** of the **n1**-th stack location (not counting the cell occupied by **n1**). The operand **n1** must be greater than zero.

The sequence **2 PICK** is equivalent to **OVER**, and **1 PICK** gives the same result as **DUP**.

Reference: 1.4

PREV   <f>

Stack: **> > > addr**

System variable containing a pointer to the header of the mass storage buffer which most recently received data from the disk. At execution, the location of the pointer will be left on the stack.

Reference: 10.2

QUERY   <f,s>

Transfer a text string from the terminal to the input buffer. Transfer continues until 80 characters have been input, or a "return" keypress is detected. One or more "null" characters (ASCII 00) are appended to the end of the text string.

Fig-FORTH will set the input offset user variable **IN** to zero.

Reference: 9.4

Colon Definition:
: QUERY
   TIB @   Leave a pointer to the start of the
                                    terminal input buffer.

   80 EXPECT   Accept up to 80 characters from the
                                      terminal to the buffer.

   0 IN !   Set user variable **IN** to zero.
 ;   Terminate definition.

QUIT   <f,s>

Restart the interpreter loop. The return stack pointer is reset to its initial value, and control is returned to the terminal for further input.

Reference: 12.2, 12.3, 12.4

Colon Definition:
: QUIT

0 BLK !	Set the user variable to denote input from the terminal.
[COMPILE] [	Suspend compilation and re-enter the execution state.
BEGIN	Begin an indefinite loop.
RP!	Reset the return stack pointer.
CR	Output a carriage return and line feed.
QUERY	Accept up to 80 characters from the terminal to the input buffer, and reset the input offset pointer.
INTERPRET	Interpret a line of text.
STATE @ 0=	True if executing.
IF ." OK" ENDIF	If executing, send a message to indicate successful interpretation of the input stream.
AGAIN	Repeat the loop unconditionally.
;	Terminate definition.

R   <f>

Stack: > > > n

Leave a copy of the top single-precision return stack value **n** on the parameter stack.
    See **R@**.

Reference: 6.8

R# (r-sharp)   <f>

Stack: > > > **addr**

User variable containing a pointer to an editing cursor or other installation-dependent file function. At execution, the location of the pointer within the user area will be left on the stack.

R/W (r-w)   <f>

Stack: **addr n f** > > >

Installation-dependent routine to transmit one block of data between a mass storage buffer and the disk. Block number **n** will be read from the disk if **f** is true, or written to the disk if **f** is false. The associated mass storage buffer's header is at **addr**.

R/W must be defined to determine the physical location of block **n**, specified as an absolute offset from the start of disk 0, and to perform any required error checking.

Reference: 10.1, 10.3

R0 (r-zero)   <f>

Stack: > > > **addr**

User variable containing the initial return stack pointer value. At execution, the location of the pointer within the user area will be left on the stack.

Reference: 6.8, 6.9

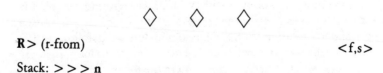

R> (r-from)   <f,s>

Stack: > > > **n**

Move the top single-precision value **n** from the return stack to the parameter stack.

Within a colon definition, use of **R>** must be balanced by **>R**. If used within a compilation structure such as a loop or conditional, both **R>** and **>R** must appear within the same nesting level.

Reference: 6.8, 12.4

R@ (r-fetch)   <s>

Stack: > > > **n**

Leave a copy of the top return stack value **n** on the parameter stack. See **R**.

Reference: 6.8

REPEAT   <f,s>

Stack: **addr1 n1 addr2 n2** > > >   (compilation)

Format: **:** <name> ... **BEGIN** ... **WHILE** ... **REPEAT** ... **;**

Immediate word to complete compilation of an indefinite loop which contains a mid-pass test for execution completion.

During compilation of <name>'s dictionary definition, **REPEAT** executes immediately due to its precedence bit. The location **addr2** is used to calculate and recompile the dummy forward offset left by **WHILE**. A pointer to the run-time unconditional branching routine is compiled into the next location in <name>'s parameter field. The location **addr1** left by **BEGIN** is used to calculate the offset back to the top of the loop and compile it following the run-time pointer. Operands **n1** and **n2** are error check values.

During later execution of <name>, the conditional branching run-time routine associated with **WHILE** will test and remove the top stack value as a flag. If the flag is false, the first offset will be used to transfer execution to the next component word following the loop. If true, execution will continue to the end of the loop, then use the second offset to transfer execution to the top of the loop.

Reference: 5.4, 12.4

Colon Definition:
: REPEAT

>R >R	Move **addr2** and **n2** to the return stack.
[COMPILE] AGAIN	Use **AGAIN**, **addr1** and **n1** to compile the run-time unconditional branch routine and an offset back to the top of the loop.
R> R>	Move **addr2** and **n2** back from the return stack.
2 −	Adjust error check value **n2**.
[COMPILE] ENDIF	Use **ENDIF** to recompile the dummy offset at **addr2**.
; IMMEDIATE	Terminate definition, set precedence.

ROLL   <s>

Stack: **n > > >**

Shift the first (not counting **n**) through the (**n−1**)-th stack values one position lower, and place the **n**-th location's original value on top of the stack. The value **n** must be greater than zero.

The sequence **3 ROLL** is equivalent to **ROT**, and **2 ROLL** to **SWAP**. The sequence **1 ROLL** has no net effect.

Reference: 1.4

ROT (rote)   <f,s>

Stack: **n1 n2 n3 > > > n2 n3 n1**

Rotate the top three values on the stack, leaving the original third value on top.

Reference: 1.4

Colon Definition:
: ROT
```
  >R              Move n3 to the return stack.
  SWAP            Exchange positions of n1 and n2.
  R>              Move n3 back to the parameter stack.
  SWAP            Exchange positions of n1 and n3.
  ;               Terminate definition.
```

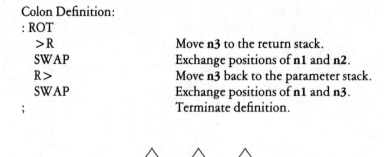

RP! (r-p-store)   <f>

Initialize the return stack pointer to the value found in user variable **R0**.

Reference: 6.8

RP@ (r-p-fetch)   <z>

Stack: > > > **addr**

Leave the current return stack pointer on the parameter stack.

Reference: 6.8

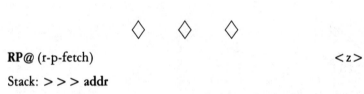

S-> D (s-to-d)   <f>

Stack: **n** > > > **d**

Convert the signed single-precision value **n** to its double-precision equivalent, with the same magnitude and sign.

Reference: 2.3

S0 (s-zero)   <f>

Stack: > > > **addr**

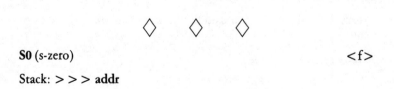

User variable containing the initial parameter stack pointer value. At execution, the location of the pointer within the user area will be left on the stack.

Reference: 1.4.5, 4.3.6, 6.7, 6.9

SAVE-BUFFERS   <s>

Write the contents of all mass storage buffers which have been marked as updated to the disk. An error condition results if disk access is not completed.
    See **FLUSH**.

Reference: 10.3, 11.3

SCR (s-c-r)   <f,s>

Stack: > > > addr

User variable containing the number of the source code screen most recently referenced by **LIST**. At execution, the location of the value within the user area will be left on the stack.

Reference: 11.2

SEC   <z>

Stack: > > > addr

System variable containing the number of the disk sector (relative to the start of the current drive) most recently referenced. At execution, the location of the value will be left on the stack.

SEC-READ   <z>

Installation-dependent routine to read a disk sector into memory. If a read error occurs, a true flag will be left in system variable

DISK-ERROR. Successful completion will store a false flag.

The drive, track, sector, and buffer address must have been previously set by **SET-DRIVE** and **SET-IO**.

Reference: 10.1

SEC-WRITE   <z>

Installation-dependent routine to write a sector from memory to disk. If a write error occurs, a true flag will be left in system variable **DISK-ERROR**. Successful completion will store a false flag.

The drive, track, sector, and buffer address must have been previously set to **SET-DRIVE** and **SET-IO**.

Reference: 10.1

SEC/BLK (sec-block)   <z>

Stack: > > > **n**

System constant to leave the number of disk sectors per block.

SET-DRIVE   <z>

Installation-dependent routine to force later disk I/O to use the drive specified by **DRIVE**.

SET-IO (set-i-o)   <z>

Installation-dependent routine to force later disk I/O to use the drive, track, and sector specified by **T&SCALC** and the mass storage buffer pointed to by **USE**.

Reference: 10.1

SIGN   <f,s>

Stack: **n ud > > > ud**   <f>
        n > > >   <s>

Format: **< # ... SIGN ... #>**

If **n** is negative, insert a negative sign character into the next location of a pictured numeric output string.

Reference: 9.5

Colon Definition:
: SIGN

ROT	Exchange positions of **n** and **ud**.
0 <	True if **n** is negative.
IF	True branch—**n** is negative.
45 HOLD	Insert a negative sign in the next character location.
ENDIF	Terminate conditional.
;	Terminate definition.

SMUDGE   <f>

Toggle the smudge bit in the length byte of the most recently created header. A header compiled by the fig-FORTH version of **CREATE** has a toggled smudge bit, which must be reset before the word may be located during a dictionary search.

Reference: 8.1

Colon Definition:
: SMUDGE

LATEST	Leave the name field address of the most recent addition to the current vocabulary.
32 TOGGLE	Toggle the smudge bit in the length byte, using the constant (20H).
;	Terminate definition.

◇   ◇   ◇

SP! (s-p-store)   <f>

Initialize the parameter stack pointer to the value found in user variable **S0**.

Reference: 6.7

◇   ◇   ◇

SP@ (s-p-fetch)   <f>

Stack: > > > **addr**

Leave the current parameter stack pointer.

Reference: 1.2, 1.4.5, 4.3.6, 6.7

◇   ◇   ◇

SPACE   <f,s>

Output a "blank" character to the terminal.

Reference: 3.3, 9.3

Colon Definition:
: SPACE
    BL   Leave the ASCII value for a blank.
    EMIT   Output the character.
  ;   Terminate definition.

◇   ◇   ◇

SPACES   <f,s>

Stack: **n** > > >

Output **n** "blank" characters to the terminal. For some versions, no spaces will be output if **n** is less than 1.

Reference: 3.3, 9.3

Colon Definition:
: SPACES

0 MAX	Leave the maximum of zero or **n**.
–DUP	Duplicate the non-zero count.
IF	True branch — non-zero count.
0	Leave an initial index value.
DO SPACE LOOP	Output the proper number of "blank" characters.
ENDIF	Terminate conditional.
;	Terminate definition.

◇ ◇ ◇

STATE   <f,s>

Stack: > > > **addr**

User variable containing the compilation state flag. An installation-dependent non-zero value denotes compilation; a false flag (zero) indicates execution. At execution, the location of the flag within the user area will be left on the stack.

Reference: 4.3, 5.5, 6.9, 12.2

◇ ◇ ◇

SWAP   <f,s>

Stack: **n1 n2 > > > n2 n1**

Exchange the positions of the top two stack values.

Reference: 1.4

◇ ◇ ◇

T&SCALC (t-and-s-calc)   <z>

Stack: **n > > >**

Installation-dependent routine to calculate the drive, track, and sector for the disk containing sector **n** (specified as an absolute sector offset from the start of drive 0).

The track and sector numbers are stored in **TRACK** and **SEC** respectively. If the calculated drive number differs from the contents of **DRIVE**, the user variable is updated and the **SET-DRIVE** routine is executed.

TASK   <f>

A null operation word used to delimit an application from the core dictionary. The application program may be eliminated by the sequence **FORGET TASK**.

Reference: 6.3

Colon Definition:
: TASK
;   Terminate definition.

THEN   <f,s>

Stack: **addr n** > > >   (compilation)

Formats: **: <name>** ... IF ... **THEN** ... ;
        : <name> ... IF ... ELSE ... **THEN** ... ;

Immediate word to complete compilation of a conditional. Equivalent to **ENDIF**.

During compilation of <name>'s dictionary definition, **THEN** executes immediately due to its precedence bit. The dummy offset previously compiled by **IF** or **ELSE** at **addr** is replaced with the actual offset from **addr** to the current dictionary location. The operand **n** is an error check value.

During later execution of <name>, the conditional branching routine associated with **IF** will test and remove the top stack value as a flag. If true, the components of the true branch will be executed; the remainder of the conditional, if any, will be ignored. If the flag is false, the initial offset will be used to transfer execution to the false branch; if no false branch exists, the true branch will simply be ignored.

Reference: 5.2, 12.4

Colon Definition:
: THEN
    [COMPILE] ENDIF   Use the equivalent definition.
; IMMEDIATE   Terminate definition, set precedence.

TIB (t-i-b)   \<f\>

Stack: > > > **addr**

User variable containing a pointer to the start of the terminal input buffer. At execution, the location of the pointer within the user area will be placed on the stack.

Reference: 6.8, 6.9

TOGGLE   \<f\>

Stack: **addr b** > > >

Perform a bit-by-bit logical "exclusive or" on the contents of **addr** and the top stack value **b**, and leave the result at **addr**.

Reference: 2.5

TRACK   \<z\>

Stack: > > > **addr**

System variable containing the number of the disk track (relative to the start of the current drive) most recently referenced. At execution, the location of the value will be left on the stack.

TRAVERSE   \<f\>

Stack: **addr1 n** > > > **addr2**

Leave a pointer **addr2** to the opposite end of the name field that begins (**n=1**) or ends (**n=−1**) at **addr1**. The beginning location holds the length byte, and the ending location contains the last stored name character. Only these locations within the name field have high-order bits set to 1.

Reference: 8.1

Colon Definition:
: TRAVERSE

SWAP	Exchange positions of **addr1** and **n**.
BEGIN	Begin an indefinite loop.
OVER	Copy **n** to the top of the stack.
+	Increment the address pointer by **n**.
127	Leave a comparison value (7FH).
OVER C@	Fetch the next character byte.
<	Leave a true flag if the high-order bit is set.
UNTIL	Repeat the loop until true.
SWAP DROP	Drop **n** from the stack.
;	Terminate definition.

TRIAD   <f>

Stack: **n** > > >

Output the ASCII text of three source code screens, including screen **n** and beginning with a screen number evenly divisible by three. The screen number user variable **SCR** is updated, and the numeric I/O base is set to decimal. A reference message (equivalent to error message 15) will be output at the completion of execution.

In some versions of fig-FORTH, the output may be prematurely ended by the terminal's "break" key.

Reference: 11.2, B.1

Colon Definition:
: TRIAD

12 EMIT	Output a form feed (0CH) character.
3 / 3 *	Calculate the number of the first screen to be output.
3 OVER + SWAP	Leave the loop limit and index values.
DO	Begin an indexed loop.
CR	Output a carriage return and line feed.
I LIST	Output one screen.
LOOP	Terminate indexed loop.
CR 15 MESSAGE CR	Output message number and, if disk is available, text line.
;	Terminate definition.

◇   ◇   ◇

TYPE   `<f,s>`

Stack: **addr n** > > >

Output a string of **n** characters, beginning with the character at **addr**. No text will be sent if **n** is less than one.

Reference: 7.3, 9.3

Colon Definition:
: TYPE

—DUP	Duplicate a non-zero count as a flag.
IF	True branch — non-zero count.
OVER + SWAP	Calculate the limit and initial loop pointers.
DO	Begin an indexed loop.
I C@ EMIT	Output one text character.
LOOP	Terminate indexed loop.
ELSE	False branch — zero count.
DROP	Drop the address pointer.
ENDIF	Terminate conditional.
;	Terminate definition.

◇   ◇   ◇

U* (u-times)   `<f,s>`

Stack: **u1 u2** > > > **u3**

Leave the unsigned product **u3** of **u1** and **u2**.

Reference: 2.4

◇   ◇   ◇

U. (u-dot)   `<z,s>`

Stack: **u** > > >

Output an unsigned single-precision value **u** to the terminal, followed by one space.

Reference: 2.1, 3.3

Colon Definition:
: U.
  0   Leave a dummy high-order half.
  D.   Output the resulting double-
                              precision number, followed by one
                              space.
  ;   Terminate definition.

U/ (u-divide)   <f>

Stack: **ud u1** > > > **u2 u3**

    Leave the unsigned remainder **u2** and quotient **u3** of the unsigned
double-precision number **ud** divided by **u1**.
  See **U/MOD**.

Reference: 2.4

U/MOD (u-divide-mod)   <s>

Stack: **ud u1** > > > **u2 u3**

    Leave the unsigned remainder **u2** and quotient **u3** of the unsigned
double-precision number **ud** divided by **u1**.
  See **U/**.

Reference: 2.4

U< (u-less-than)   <z,s>

Stack: **u1 u2** > > > **f**

    Leave a true flag if the unsigned value **u1** is less than **u2**. Other-
wise, use a false flag. Memory addresses must be compared using
U< rather than **<**.

Reference: 5.1

◇   ◇   ◇

UNTIL   \<f,s>

Stack: **f** > > >   (run-time)
    addr n > > >   (compilation)

Format: **:** \<name> ... **BEGIN** ... **UNTIL** ... **;**

Immediate word to complete compilation of an indefinite loop which contains a post-pass test for execution completion. Equivalent to **END**.

During compilation of \<name>'s dictionary definition, **UNTIL** executes immediately due to its precedence bit. A pointer to the run-time conditional branching routine is compiled into \<name>'s parameter field. The location **addr** left by **BEGIN** is used to calculate and compile an offset back to the top of the loop. The **n** operand is used as an error check value.

During later execution of \<name>, the conditional branching run-time routine associated with **UNTIL** will test and remove the top stack value **f**. If the flag is true, execution continues with the next component word following the loop. If the flag is false, the offset will be used to transfer execution to the top of the loop.

Reference: 5.4, 12.4

Colon Definition:
: UNTIL

1 ?PAIRS	Test the error check value **n**. If not equal to 1, issue an error message.
COMPILE 0BRANCH	Compile a pointer to the run-time routine in the next available dictionary location.
BACK	Use **addr** to calculate and compile the backward offset to the top of the loop.
; IMMEDIATE	Terminate definition, set precedence.

◇   ◇   ◇

UPDATE   \<f,s>

Mark the contents of the mass storage buffer most recently read from the disk as updated. If the buffer is later needed to contain another block of data, the contents of the buffer will first be written back to the disk.

Reference: 10.2, 10.3

Colon Definition:
: UPDATE
   PREV @   Leave a pointer to the header of the
                                 most recently referenced buffer.
   @   Fetch the header contents.
   32768 OR   Set the high-order bit to 1, using the
                                 constant (8000H).
   PREV @   Leave the pointer again.
   !   Store the header bytes.
;   Terminate definition.

USE   \<f\>

Stack: > > > **addr**

System variable containing a pointer to the header of the mass storage buffer least recently used. At execution, the location of the pointer will be left on the stack.

Reference: 10.2

USER   \<f\>

Stack: **n** > > >

Format: **USER** \<**name**\>

Defining word used to create a dictionary entry for \<**name**\> containing the offset pointer **n** in its parameter field. When \<**name**\> is later executed, a pointer to the location **n** bytes above the start of the user area will be left on the stack.

Reference: 3.2, 6.9, 7.2, 8.3

Colon Definition:
: USER

CONSTANT	Compile a dictionary entry for the next word < name > taken from the input stream, and a parameter field containing the value n.
;CODE mn	Terminate compilation of **USER** by compiling a pointer to the associated run-time procedure and the machine code corresponding to mnemonics **mn**. When **USER** is later executed, the code field of < name > will be changed to point to the generic procedure specified by **mn**.

VARIABLE   <f,s>

Stack: **n** > > >   <f>

Format: **VARIABLE** < name >

Defining word used to create a dictionary entry for < name > to contain a variable value in its parameter field.

A significant difference exists between fig-FORTH and FORTH-79 versions. Fig-FORTH will store the initial value **n** in < name >'s dictionary definition during compilation. A variable compiled with the FORTH-79 version must be explicitly initialized after compilation.

When < name > is later executed, the location of its value will be placed on the stack.

VARIABLE should not be used as a component in a colon definition.

Reference: 3.2, 4.1, 4.2, 7.2, 8.3

Colon Definition:
: VARIABLE

CONSTANT	Compile a dictionary entry for the next word < name > taken from the input stream, and a parameter field containing the value n.
;CODE mn	Terminate compilation of **VARIABLE**

by compiling a pointer to the
associated run-time procedure and
the machine code corresponding to
mnemonics **mn**. When **VARIABLE**
is later executed, the code field of
< **name** > will be changed to point
to the generic procedure specified
by **mn**.

VLIST   < f >

Output a list of the words within the context vocabulary, ordered
from newest to oldest. The output may be ended prematurely by the
terminal's "break" key.

Reference: 7.1

Colon Definition:
```
: VLIST
  128 OUT !              Initialize the output offset pointer.
  CONTEXT @ @            Fetch the name field address of the
                            most recent addition to the context
                            vocabulary.

  BEGIN                  Begin an indefinite loop.
    OUT @                Fetch the output offset pointer.
    C/L >                True if the offset is greater than the
                            standard line length.

    IF                   True branch—end of line.
      CR                 Output a carriage return.
      0 OUT !            Reset the offset pointer.
    ENDIF                Terminate conditional.
    DUP                  Duplicate the name field pointer.
    ID. SPACE SPACE      Output the name, followed by two
                            spaces.
    PFA LFA              Leave the link field address.
    @                    Fetch the pointer to the next most
                            recent word's name field.
    DUP 0=               True if the vocabulary has been
                            exhausted.
```

?TERMINAL	True if "break" detected.
OR	True if either of the prior two flags was true.
UNTIL	Continue the loop until a true flag.
DROP	Drop the remaining pointer.
;	Terminate definition.

◇   ◇   ◇

VOC-LINK   <f>

Stack: > > > **addr**

User variable containing a pointer to a parameter in the most recently created vocabulary's defining word. Used to **FORGET** through multiple vocabularies. At execution, the location of the pointer within the user area will be left on the stack.

Reference: 6.9, 7.4

◇   ◇   ◇

VOCABULARY   <f,s>

Format: **VOCABULARY** <vname> **IMMEDIATE**

Defining word used to initiate a linked list of definitions for the <vname> vocabulary.

When executed, **VNAME** will create a header for <vname> linked to the current vocabulary. Later execution of <vname>, which is an immediate word, will make <vname> the context vocabulary in which all dictionary searches begin. Execution of the sequence

<vname> **DEFINITIONS**

will make <vname> the current vocabulary as well, in which new definitions will be placed.

All user-defined vocabularies are linked to **FORTH**. For fig-FORTH, each vocabulary is also linked to its "trunk" vocabulary in which <vname> is defined, and the various "trunks" of that vocabulary as well.

VOCABULARY should not be used as a component in colon definitions.

Reference: 7.1, 7.4

Colon Definition:
: VOCABULARY

<BUILDS	Compile a definition using the high-level defining word.
41089 ,	Compile a dummy constant (0A081H) in the first usable parameter field location.
CURRENT @	Fetch the pointer to the current vocabulary's defining word.
CFA ,	Decrement the pointer by 2 and compile it into the new parameter field.
HERE	Leave the current dictionary pointer.
VOC-LINK @ ,	Fetch and compile the vocabulary linkage pointer.
VOC-LINK !	Store the pointer's location in the user variable.
DOES>	Specify execution behavior.
2+	Increment the parameter field address by 2.
CONTEXT !	Update the context vocabulary pointer.
;	Terminate definition.

WARNING   <f>

Stack: > > > **addr**

  User variable containing a value specifying the error message mode. If the value equals 1, error messages are taken from the disk, beginning with line 0 of screen 4 on drive 0 (regardless of the currently enabled drive). If equal to 0, only a message number is output. A value of −1 causes the user-definable **(ABORT)** routine to be executed when an error condition is found.

  At execution, the location of the value within the user area will be left on the stack.

Reference: 6.9, 12.4, B.1

◇   ◇   ◇

WHILE   <f,s>

Stack: f > > >   (run-time)
    addr1 n1 > > > addr1 n1
            addr2 n2   (compilation)

Format: : < name > ... **BEGIN** ... **WHILE** ... **REPEAT** ... ;

   Immediate word to continue compilation of an indefinite loop which contains a mid-pass test for execution completion.

   During compilation of < name >'s dictionary entry, **WHILE** executes immediately due to its precedence bit. The parameters **addr1** and **n1** were previously left on the stack by **BEGIN**. A pointer to the run-time conditional branching routine is compiled into the next location in < name >'s parameter field, along with a dummy forward offset pointer at **addr2**. The result **n2** is an error check value.

   During later execution of < name >, the conditional branching run-time routine associated with **WHILE** will test and remove the top stack value f as a flag. If the flag is false, the offset at **addr2** will be used to transfer execution to the next component word following the loop. If true, execution will continue to the end of the loop, then use the run-time routine and offset compiled by **REPEAT** to transfer execution to the top of the loop.

Reference: 5.4, 12.4

Colon Definition:
: WHILE
   [COMPILE] IF   Use **IF** to compile the run-time
                              conditional branching routine, and
                              a dummy pointer at **addr2**, then
                              leave **addr2** and an error check
                              value.
     2+   Increment **n2**.
; IMMEDIATE   Terminate definition, set precedence.

◇   ◇   ◇

WIDTH   <f>

Stack: > > > addr

User variable containing the maximum number $(1-31)$ of characters which may be stored in a dictionary definition's name field. The original length (up to 31) is saved in the length byte, and the characters (up to the number specified by the user variable) immediately follow, truncated as necessary. At execution, the location of the number within the user area will be left on the stack.

Reference: 3.2.4, 4.2.1, 6.9, 7.2, 8.1

WORD   <f,s>

Stack: c > > >   <f>
    c > > > addr   <s>

Parse the next word, delimited by a trailing character **c**, from the input stream. Leading delimiter **c** characters will be ignored, while a "null" will be treated as an absolute delimiter. The input stream is denoted by the value of user variable **BLK**.

Significant differences exist between the fig-FORTH and FORTH-79 versions. The fig-FORTH version copies the word, with a leading count byte and two or more (uncounted) trailing blanks, to the word buffer. FORTH-79 copies the dimensioned string to memory beginning at **addr**, followed by the actual delimiter (**c** or "null") found in the input stream. If the input stream is exhausted, a zero count results.

Colon Definition:
: WORD
   BLK @   Fetch the input block number.
   IF   True branch — input from disk.
      BLK @   Fetch the block number again.
      BLOCK   Leave the buffer address of the block,
              reading it from the disk if not
              already in memory.
   ELSE   False branch — input from terminal.
     TIB @   Fetch a pointer to the input buffer.
   ENDIF   Terminate conditional.
   IN @ +   Leave a pointer to the next character
              to be checked in the input or mass
              storage buffer.
   SWAP   Exchange positions of pointer and c.

ENCLOSE	Leave the original pointer, a byte offset to the first non-delimiter, another to the first delimiter after a valid character, and the next character to be checked.
HERE 34 BLANKS	Fill the first 34 bytes of the word buffer with blanks.
IN +!	Increment the offset pointer to the next character to be checked.
OVER –	Calculate the length of the string between delimiters.
>R R	Save a copy of the length on the return stack.
HERE C!	Compile the count in the first byte of the word buffer.
+	Leave the absolute address of the first non-delimiter in the input or mass storage buffer.
HERE 1+	Leave the address of the next word buffer location after the count byte.
R>	Move the count back from the return stack.
CMOVE	Copy the string from the input or mass storage buffer to the word buffer.
;	Terminate definition.

◇   ◇   ◇

XOR (x-or)   <f,s>

Stack: **n1 n2 > > > n3**

Leave the bit-by-bit logical "exclusive or" **n3** of **n1** and **n2**. The i-th bit of **n3** will be set to 1 only if the i-th bit of **n1** or the i-th bit of **n2** (but not both) is 1.

Reference: 2.5

◇   ◇   ◇

[(left-bracket)   <f,s>

Immediate word to suspend compilation and set the **STATE** user

variable to denote execution. Until the user variable is again
changed, subsequent words in the input stream will be executed
rather than compiled.

Reference: 5.5

Colon Definition:
: [
   0 STATE !   Store a zero in the user variable.
; IMMEDIATE   Terminate definition, set precedence.

[COMPILE] (bracket-compile)   <f,s>

Format: : < name > ... **[COMPILE]** < name1 > ... ;

Immediate word to force compilation of the immediate word
< name1 > as a component in the definition of < name >. The
word < name1 > will only be executed during execution of
< name >, rather than during compilation of that definition.

Reference: 5.5, B.1

Colon Definition:
: [COMPILE]
   –FIND   Copy the next blank-delimited word
                         from the input stream to the word
                         buffer, and search the current and
                         context vocabularies for a match. If
                         found, leave the word's parameter
                         field address, the contents of its
                         name field length byte, and a true
                         flag; otherwise leave only a false
                         flag.
   0= 0 ?ERROR   If no match found, issue an error
                         message.
   DROP   Drop the length byte contents.
   CFA   Leave the code field address of
                         < name1 >.
   ,   Compile the pointer into the next
                         location in < name >'s parameter
                         field.
; IMMEDIATE   Terminate definition, set precedence.

] (right-bracket)   < f,s >

Resume compilation within a colon definition, and set the **STATE** user variable to denote compilation. Until the user variable is again changed, subsequent non-immediate words in the input stream will be compiled rather than executed.

The value stored in **STATE** may be installation-dependent.

Reference: 5.5

Colon Definition:
:]
    192 STATE !   Store a value (0C0H) denoting
                              compilation in the user variable.
  ;   Terminate definition.

ABOUT THE AUTHOR

C. Kevin McCabe is a trial attorney with the Chicago/Los Angeles/Atlanta firm of Lord, Bissell & Brook, where he specializes in aviation accident litigation. His earlier work as an aeronautical and astronautical engineer included fundamental research on commercial wind turbines, and development of flight control systems for NASA's Space Shuttle. He is a Sponsor of the FORTH Standards Team, and a Member of the FORTH Interest Group. His other publications include numerous articles in *Microcomputing, Dr. Dobb's Journal, Air Progress,* and major newspapers, as well as two other textbooks available from dilithium Press.

MORE HELPFUL WORDS
FOR YOU from dilithium Press

Bits, Bytes and Buzzwords
Mark Garetz

This book translates all the computer jargon you've been hearing into words you can understand. It explains microcomputers, software and peripherals in a way that makes sense, so your buying decisions are easier and smarter.

ISBN 0-88056-111-4   *160 pages*   *$7.95*

Computers For Everybody, 3rd Edition
Jerry Willis and Merl Miller

In a clear, understandable way, this new edition explains how a computer can be used in your home, office or at school. If you're anxious to buy a computer, use one, or just want to find out about them, read this book first!

ISBN 0-88056-131-9   *200 pages*   *$7.95*

Instant (Freeze-Dried Computer Programming in) BASIC—2nd Astounding! Edition
Jerald R. Brown

Here is an active, easy, painless way to learn BASIC. This primer and workbook gives you a fast, working familiarity with the real basics of BASIC. It is one of the smoothest and best-tested instructional sequences going!

ISBN 0-918398-57-6   *200 pages*   *$12.95*

Are You Computer Literate?
Karen Billings and David Moursund

This is a fun introduction to computers for the real novice. Written by educators, it is a book that teaches the capabilities, limitations, applications and implications of computers.

ISBN 0-918398-29-0   *160 pages*   *$9.95*

BRAINFOOD — Our catalog listing of over 130 microcomputer books covering software, hardware, business applications, general computer literacy and programming languages.

dilithium Press books are available at your local bookstore or computer store. If there is not a bookstore or computer store in your area, charge your order on VISA or MC by calling our toll-free number, (800) 547-1842.

Send to: dilithium Press, P.O. Box E, Beaverton, OR 97075
Please send me the book(s) I have checked. I understand that if I'm not fully satisfied I can return the book(s) within 10 days for full and prompt refund.

____ Bits, Bytes and Buzzwords

____ Computers For Everybody, 3rd Edition

____ Instant (Freeze-Dried Computer Programming in) BASIC—2nd Astounding! Edition
____ Are You Computer Literate?

☐ Check enclosed $ _____
   Payable to dilithium Press

☐ Please charge my
   VISA ☐   MASTERCHARGE ☐

   # _____ Exp. Date _____

Name_____

Address_____

City, State, Zip _____

Signature _____

☐ Send me your catalog, Brainfood.

☐ **Yes, send me your free catalog, BRAINFOOD, which lists over 130 microcomputer books covering software, hardware, business applications, general computer literacy and programming languages.**

NAME _____

ADDRESS _____

CITY, STATE, ZIP _____

☐ **Yes, send me your free catalog, BRAINFOOD, which lists over 130 microcomputer books covering software, hardware, business applications, general computer literacy and programming languages.**

NAME _____

ADDRESS _____

CITY, STATE, ZIP _____

☐ **Yes, send me your free catalog, BRAINFOOD, which lists over 130 microcomputer books covering software, hardware, business applications, general computer literacy and programming languages.**

NAME _____

ADDRESS _____

CITY, STATE, ZIP _____

FREE CATALOG FREE CATALOG FREE CATA LOG FREE CATALOG FREE CATALOG FREE CATALOG FREE CATA LOG FREE CATALOG FREE CATALOG FREE CATALOG FREE CATA LOG FREE CATALOG FREE CATALOG FREE CATALOG FREE CATA LOG FREE CATALOG FREE CATALOG FREE CATALOG FREE CATA LOG FREE CATALOG FREE CATALOG FREE CATALOG FREE CATA LOG FREE CATALOG FREE CATALOG FREE CATALOG FREE CATA LOG FREE CATALOG

Mail To:

dilithium Press
P.O. Box E
Beaverton, OR 97075

Or Call:

800-547-1842

FREE CATALOG FREE CATALOG FREE CATA LOG FREE CATALOG FREE CATALOG FREE CATALOG FREE CATA LOG FREE CATALOG FREE CATALOG FREE CATALOG FREE CATA LOG FREE CATALOG FREE CATALOG FREE CATALOG FREE CATA LOG FREE CATALOG FREE CATALOG FREE CATALOG FREE CATA LOG FREE CATALOG FREE CATALOG FREE CATALOG FREE CATA LOG FREE CATALOG FREE CATALOG FREE CATALOG FREE CATA LOG FREE CATALOG FREE CATALOG FREE